InStyle
PARTIES

InStyle
PARTIES

The Complete Guide
to Easy, Elegant Entertaining
All Year Round

By the editors of InStyle

Oxmoor
House®

©2017 Time Inc. Books
Published by Oxmoor House, an imprint
of Time Inc. Books
225 Liberty Street, New York, NY 10281

Assistant Editor: April Smitherman Colburn
Project Editor: Melissa Brown
Design Director: Melissa Clark
Designer: AnnaMaria Jacob
Photo Director: Paden Reich
Photographers: Alison Miksch, Time Inc. Food Studios
Prop Stylists: Thom Driver, Time Inc. Food Studios
Food Stylists: Ana Kelly, Time Inc. Food Studios
Recipe Developers and Testers: Betsy Reynolds Bateson,
    Sunset Publishing Corp. (sunset.com); Carla Hall;
    Jackie Mills, R.D.; Kate Parham; Jan Jacks Potter;
    Sara Quessenberry; Raeanne Sarazen;
    Coastal Living Test Kitchen; *Cooking Light* Test Kitchen;
    Food & Wine Test Kitchen; Oxmoor House Test Kitchen;
    Southern Living Test Kitchen; Time Inc. Food Studios
Senior Production Manager: Greg A. Amason
Assistant Production Manager: Kelsey Smith
Copy Editor: Donna Baldone
Proofreader: Rebecca Brennan
Fellows: Kaitlyn Pacheco, Holly Ravazzolo

ISBN-13: 978-0-8487-5230-9
Library of Congress Control Number: 2017944518

First Edition 2017

Printed in the United States of America

10 9 8 7 6 5 4 3 2 1

We welcome your comments and suggestions about Time Inc. Books. Please write to us at:
Time Inc. Books
Attention: Book Editors
P.O. Box 62310
Tampa, Florida 33662-2310

Time Inc. Books products may be purchased for business or promotional use. For information on bulk purchases, please contact Christi Crowley in the Special Sales Department at (845) 895-9858.

Publisher Credits:
Seared Salmon with White Beans & Spinach (p. 62) from *STIR: Mixing It Up In the Italian Tradition* by Barbara Lynch. Copyright © 2009 by Barbara Lynch. Used by permission of Houghton Mifflin Harcourt. All rights reserved.

Herb Tartines (p. 90) from *Nature: Simple, Healthy and Good*, by Alain Ducasse. Rizzoli International Publications, Inc., 2012.

Mini Cherry Cheesecakes with Oreo Crust (p. 91) from The New Potato. Mini Cherry Cheesecakes with Oreo Crust. January 5, 2016. http://www.thenewpotato.com/2016/01/05/cherry-cheesecake-recipe-with-oreo-crust/.

Chocolate Tart with Pine Nut Crust (p. 116) from *Gjelina* © 2015 by Travis Lett. Used with permission of Chronicle Books LLC, San Francisco. Visit ChronicleBooks.com.

Frankies Lemonade (p. 160); Frankies Corn Salad (p. 162); Tomato, Avocado & Red Onion Salad (p. 162); Grilled Vegetables (p. 163); Slow-Roasted Rib Eye, Sliced Cold (p. 163); Olive Oil Cake with Berries & Cream (p. 163) adapted from *The Frankies Spuntino Kitchen Companion & Cooking Manual*. Copyright © 2010 by Frank Falcinelli, Frank Castronovo, and Peter Meehan. Used by permission of Workman Publishing Co., Inc., New York. All Rights Reserved.

Strawberry-Basil Sangria (p. 176) reprinted from the book *Malibu Farm Cookbook: Recipes from the California Coast*. Copyright © 2016 by Martin Lof. Published by arrangement with Clarkson Potter/Publishers, an imprint of Crown Publishing Group, a division of Penguin Random House LLC.

Spice-Rubbed Fish Sliders (p. 178); Kale, Chickpea, Fennel & Date Salad (p. 179); Pear, Ginger & Thyme Tarte Tatin (p. 179) from *Bondi Harvest: Seasonal, Sustainable, Simple, and Shareable Food* © 2015 by HarperCollins Publishers Australia. Authored by Guy Turland and Mark Alston. Photography by Stephen Baccon. Used by permission.

CONTENTS

INTRODUCTION

There's nothing like a great party, one that perfectly celebrates the occasion, expresses the creativity of its host, and serves as a joyous gift to everyone there. So, what's the secret?

While even the world's greatest entertainers don't strive for perfection, they do revel in the details, and taking the time to plan out a dinner, special occasion, or family gathering makes all the difference. As a host, you know you've done it right when the table looks vibrant and inviting, the food is irresistible, and the mood is laid-back and relaxed. But entertaining in this modern new way—using clever styling statements, the freshest ingredients, and stunningly simple recipes—means that once the guests arrive, you'll be free to join in the fun.

Within these pages you'll find everything you need to throw an affair to remember, no matter what the occasion—including the tips and tricks that will make the planning and preparation a pleasure at every step along the way.

THE
BASICS

Entertaining is a refreshingly democratic affair. It doesn't matter if you can barely boil water or if you're a talented chef, whether you live in a tiny studio or in a giant loft. With a little enthusiasm, planning, and creativity, you're capable of just about anything.

What you'll need, however, is a primer that details the essentials of invitations, food and beverages, and stylish décor. In the following pages, we start with the nitty-gritty like ice and coatracks and move on to tips for creating a buoyant, festive atmosphere in your home with flowers, lighting, and music. These elements, after all, form the foundation of every memorable celebration.

THE INVITATIONS

You can spend days, even weeks, envisioning a wonderful party: who's there, what you'll serve, where the festivities will unfold. But it isn't official until you invite the guests. You can do this in a variety of ways, ranging from a quick phone call to a beautifully printed or engraved card. Whatever the format, all invitations serve the same purpose: They set the tone for a celebration and provide guests with all the information they need. On a lighter note, they get everyone (host included) excited for a good time.

YOU'RE INVITED!

Share all the vital details while subtly setting the proper tone.

PICK THE RIGHT INVITE

Think about the kind of party you want to give and choose invitations with the same feel and formality. If it's a very casual occasion, like a dinner party or impromptu drinks with close friends, a phone call is perfectly appropriate. If you want to tell a large number of people about a last-minute gathering in your home (weekend barbecue, group viewing of a TV show finale), invite them by e-mail. For more organized or formal events (a large dinner party, cocktail party, birthday, or holiday open house), written invitations are in order. The easiest method is to send traditional fill-in-the-blank invitations. You may think of them as unimaginative, but that's an old stigma. You can also send invitations electronically. There are many online invitation sites that offer an extensive selection of digital designs that can be e-mailed to guests at little to no cost and some sites even offer the option to order paper copies of their electronic designs.

These days, plenty of stationery companies offer chic, well-designed styles customized for all kinds of occasions. Another even more classic choice is to write the information on a high-quality note card—a personalized card is ideal. Custom-printed invitations, which you order at a stationery shop, department store, or online are stylish and exciting to receive, as are hand-lettered or calligraphed invitations, like the one on page 95. These are most commonly used to celebrate a milestone birthday, anniversary, engagement, or shower. Engraved or letterpress invitations signify an extremely fancy party and a posh setting and are typically reserved for weddings. Of course, those are just guidelines. Bend the rules however you'd like, as long as the invitation clearly tells guests what to expect.

WHEN AND WHERE

Beyond making a striking first impression, the role of the party invitation is to convey facts. Here's what to include:

THE REASON FOR THE PARTY (AND WHAT FOOD AND DRINK TO EXPECT): Be as specific as possible. If the occasion is a friend's birthday, write something such as "Please join us for cake and Champagne to celebrate Lucy's 30th." (Make sure the birthday girl doesn't mind sharing her age.) If it's a cocktail party, you might say "You're invited for drinks and hors d'oeuvres." That way, people won't expect dinner.

THE DATE AND TIME: For most parties, especially dinners, a starting time is sufficient. If you want guests to leave at a certain time, include an ending time. This is most appropriate for early cocktail parties (from 6:30 P.M. to 8:30 P.M., for example), showers, brunches, and kids' parties. To avoid a crush at an open house, invite guests in staggered blocks: one set of invitations might say "3 P.M. to 6 P.M.," the next might say "4 P.M. to 7 P.M.," and so on.

THE LOCATION: If you're inviting people who have never been to your home, include a digital link to a map and/or directions.

AN RSVP LINE: Include a phone number and/or e-mail address so people can tell you whether or not they will attend. (The phrase "Regrets only" is too open-ended.) You might also list a date by which people should reply. If you don't hear from someone and the party is a few days away, follow up with a phone call.

PERFECT TIMING

There's something luxurious about looking forward to a great party. For that reason, coupled with the fact that everyone is overbooked these days, send invitations well in advance.

COMPILE YOUR GUEST LIST AT LEAST SIX WEEKS before the party. To encourage lively interaction, invite friends from different areas of your life, some who have met and some who haven't, and blend couples with single people. Mixing guests of different ages, and even generations, can also enrich the group dynamic.

FOR A SMALL COCKTAIL OR DINNER PARTY, MAIL or e-mail invitations so that guests receive them about three weeks in advance. That gives guests time to check in with a spouse or book a babysitter or clear their calendar, if need be.

FOR A MORE FORMAL OCCASION OR A BIG BASH, send invitations four to six weeks in advance. If your party is scheduled for the busy holiday season or on a major holiday (a Fourth of July picnic, for instance), call or e-mail guests a week or two before mailing the invitations and ask them to save the date.

ANY OTHER RELEVANT INFORMATION: If it's a surprise, say so on the invitation. If it's a wedding or baby shower, include registry information. Unless it's a costume party, a black-tie affair, or you want everyone to wear, say, white, don't dictate a dress code. Terms like "festive" and "creative" cause confusion. The invitation wording, style, typeface, and quality of paper should convey what to wear.

CONSIDER YOUR CROWD: For special friends, take the time to send a handwritten message along with the invitation—"It won't be the same without you. Please, come!" For those who have kids, take the time to let them know whether other children will attend the party, and their ages, or whether you'll have special kids' events or food or a babysitter on duty. Give them the relevant details to help them get there. If your guests are gluten-free, vegetarian, or allergic to some foods, let them know you've got their needs covered in advance. In consideration of guests with physical limitations, you'll need to let them know about access to the venue. And, of course, a friend recovering from a recent breakup would probably want to know if her ex will be there. In other words, run down the names on your list, thinking about what they might need in order to enjoy the party.

THE BAR

It's as predictable as Champagne on New Year's:
Upon arrival, guests always head straight to the bar.
There's a reason for this—the mere act of holding
a glass, even if it's filled with club soda, puts people
at ease. Be sure to stock the bar with a range
of tried-and-true favorites to satisfy those guests
who know exactly what they want, as well as some
fun selections for the adventurous. Here's what
you need to be ready for any occasion.

THE BASICS

Stock your bar with a smart range of must-haves and novelties that will come in handy at any event you host.

CERTAIN ESSENTIALS: Flat and sparkling water, regular and diet sodas, and lemons and limes belong in every home bar. Beyond that, the style and size of your party determine what you pour. The most basic options are wine and beer, which makes sense at casual gatherings and big parties, like open houses, where you want to keep things as streamlined as possible. For more variety, set up a modified bar with wine, beer, and a handful of standard liquors such as gin, rum, tequila, vodka, and whiskey along with mixers such as coffee, juice, and soda. And if you're hosting a true cocktail party or formal affair, set up a full bar, stocked to make any mixed drink a guest might want.

THERE'S SOME ROOM FOR VARIATION: You can add Champagne or sparkling wine to any kind of bar, and you can choose not to serve red wine or dark-colored cocktails if you have light furniture or carpeting. Make a classic cocktail party feel extra special by passing out a signature drink. If you mix a killer mojito or you're famous for your bone-dry martinis, serve them in large quantities. Otherwise, choose a cocktail that suits the mood and food of the occasion: kir royales before a French meal, mint juleps at a Kentucky Derby brunch, and margaritas or mojitos with Latin-inspired cuisine.

QUANTITIES: A 750-milliliter bottle of wine pours 4 to 6 glasses and a 750-milliliter bottle of spirits makes about 16 drinks. But for a more accurate breakdown, a salesperson at a good liquor store can fine-tune quantities by factoring in the number of guests, the length of the party, and any specific preferences you may wish to consider (say, a large contingent of bourbon or beer drinkers).

GLASSWARE

There's a specific kind of glass for every cocktail, and you can rent the whole gamut if you'd like. But it's much simpler to stock up on a few styles. Rent equal numbers of each.

ALL-PURPOSE, 11-OUNCE STEMWARE GLASS: This is suitable for red and white wine, sparkling water, sangria, and Champagne (but only in a pinch; if you love bubbly, invest in flutes). Look for one that isn't too narrow or too round. (To keep things really simple, use it for mixed drinks and sodas too.)

8- TO 10-OUNCE HIGHBALL GLASS: Ideal for water, soda, beer, and most mixed drinks.

OLD-FASHIONED: Also known as a lowball, whiskey, or rocks glass, this short tumbler is appropriate for anything on the rocks.

CLASSIC 4- TO 6-OUNCE COCKTAIL, OR MARTINI, GLASS: It's a bit disorienting to drink a martini or cosmopolitan from anything else, so invest in a set of six or eight. You'll feel glamorous every time you use them.

WHAT TO STOCK

For a cocktail party of 50, you'll be in good shape.

2 liters of **vodka**
1 small bottle (375 milliliters) of **dry vermouth** for martinis
1 liter each of **rum, scotch (blended), bourbon, tequila, triple sec,** and **gin**
1 bottle of **Rose's lime juice**
1 bottle of **Worcestershire sauce**
1 bottle of **Tabasco sauce**
2 gallons each of **orange** and **cranberry juice**
1 gallon each of **grapefruit** and **tomato juice**
6 liters each of **tonic water, seltzer, cola, diet cola,** and **club soda**
10 bottles each of **red** and **white wine**
2 cases of **beer**

GARNISHES: Stock up on lemons and limes (a dozen of each). A full bar calls for green olives, cocktail onions, maraschino cherries (a couple of jars of each), orange slices, and lemon twists. You may also need coarse salt for margaritas and celery stalks for Bloody Marys.

ICE: Make sure you have one pound of ice cubes per guest, plus lots of crushed ice to keep beer and white wine cool. Have commercial ice cubes, which stay separated, delivered the day of your party.

BARWARE

Proper accessories will keep you mixing in style.

CORKSCREW: The most practical and essential bar gadget is a "waiter's tool," which folds up like a pocketknife and combines a blade for cutting foil, a corkscrew, and a bottle opener.

ICE SCOOP: A metal ice scoop is a wise purchase. Regular spoons are too shallow or small, and tongs are frustrating.

SHAKER: The key to cold, well-mixed cocktails (and most have built-in strainers). For a big party, keep two on hand.

LONG-HANDLE SPOON: This does double duty: It stirs mixed drinks and muddles ingredients like mint leaves and lime wedges.

SMALL CHOPPING BOARD AND KNIFE: For cutting and peeling lemons and limes

SHOT GLASS OR JIGGER: Crucial for pouring accurate quantities. A shot glass holds $1\frac{1}{2}$ ounces of liquid. A jigger holds $1\frac{1}{2}$ ounces on the larger side and 1 ounce on the smaller end.

NAPKINS: Provide three paper cocktail napkins per guest; four if you're serving hors d'oeuvres.

PITCHERS: Simple, attractive glass or plastic ones for mixers

GLASSWARE: Allow three glasses per guest for a two-hour party. (For a dinner party, plan on two glasses plus the wineglasses set on the table.)

COCKTAILS

Now that the logistics of the home bar are in place, you can shift your attention to something sexier: tasty drinks. With dozens of Web sites devoted to cocktail recipes, it's a cinch to concoct anything from an appletini to a zombie. Master these six classics, and you'll be ready to make anything.

MARTINI: Fill a cocktail shaker three-fourths full with ice and pour in a splash of very dry vermouth. Shake well. Gently pour the vermouth (through the strainer, leaving the ice in the shaker) down the drain. Pour 2 ounces vodka or gin into the shaker. Shake well; pour into an ice-cold (chilled in the freezer) martini glass. Garnish with a few olives, a twist of lemon peel, or, to make a Gibson, cocktail onions.

COSMOPOLITAN: Combine 1½ ounces vodka, 1 cup ice, and ¼ ounce each of lime juice, cranberry juice, and triple sec in a cocktail shaker. Shake well and strain into an ice-cold martini glass. Garnish with a lime wedge.

CHAMPAGNE COCKTAIL: Put 1 sugar cube and 2 dashes of bitters (a bitter-tasting aromatic flavoring made of herbs and roots) into a chilled Champagne flute. Fill the glass with Champagne. A twist of lemon peel is optional.

MARGARITA: Rub the rim of a cocktail glass with a lime wedge and dip in a saucer of coarse salt. Put 1½ ounces tequila, ½ ounce triple sec, 1 ounce lime juice, and a handful of ice in a shaker (there should be enough ice that the liquid fills the shaker). Shake well and strain into the glass. Garnish with a lime slice.

SHOP AND SAVE

When buying and storing drinks, keep these practical tips in mind:

BUY IN ADVANCE. Soda stays bubbly for at least a month, beer has a shelf life of three to six months, and alcohol lasts months, even years. Store all beverages in a cool, dry place like a garage or basement.

BUY IN BULK. You'll save money and always have extra bottles around for last-minute entertaining.

DON'T BUY LIQUOR IN BIG BOTTLES. There's something tacky about hoisting a half-gallon jug of booze to make a cocktail. Even though it costs a little more, buy at least one one-liter bottle, and replenish it using the bigger bottle for parties. Smaller bottles look nicer and are easier to handle.

ASK ABOUT THE RETURN POLICY. Usually you can take back bottles that haven't been opened or chilled, but rules vary from store to store.

HAVE IT DELIVERED. A big time-saver. Schedule delivery for the evening before or the morning of the party.

CHILL WITH CARE. White wine and all mixers should be chilled when you serve them. It takes at least two hours for a bottle of wine to chill in the refrigerator. A shortcut: Fill an ice bucket (or big bowl) two-thirds full with a mixture of half ice and half water, and submerge the bottle for 25 minutes. Never put wine in the freezer (it alters the flavor and still takes longer than the bucket method), and never put chilled beer and other carbonated drinks back in room-temperature storage: The fluctuations in temperature make bubbly drinks go flat.

BLOODY MARY: Pour 3 ounces tomato juice, 1½ ounces vodka, ½ teaspoon Worcestershire sauce, 2 to 3 drops of Tabasco sauce, and a dash of lemon juice in a shaker. Add salt and pepper to taste. Add a pinch of celery salt or a few celery seeds and ½ teaspoon horseradish, if desired. Shake well and strain into a highball glass over ice cubes. Garnish with a lime wedge or celery stalk, or both.

CLASSIC SPRITZ: Layer 2 ounces bitter liqueur, 3 ounces white sparkling wine (Prosecco or cava), and 2 ounces soda water in a wineglass over ice and garnish with a citrus round. This Italian cocktail is a low-alcohol delight and can be made with whichever bitters you like, including Aperol and Campari. Use the basic formula above, and get creative with your variations.

BEER

Thanks to a surge in microbreweries and beer pubs, choices abound. There are two types of beer: lagers, which are pale, dry, light, and refreshing, and ales, which are robust, loaded with fruity and spicy flavors, and higher in alcohol content than lagers. Think about making a selection based on the party's theme. For example, for the Game Day Fiesta (page 120), you'll want to stock up on a range of great Mexican beers. At a warm-weather cookout, everyone will gravitate towards light, refreshing brews. To make the best choices, study these descriptions of the different beer types and their optimal food matches.

LAGERS

TYPE: Pilsner
TASTE: This amber-colored beer is dry, crisp, and flowery, with some bitterness.
SERVE WITH: Fried and spicy foods, as well as any kind of fish

TYPE: Pale lager
TASTE: Mild and fizzy, with no bitterness or aftertaste
SERVE WITH: Hors d'oeuvres and spicy Latin or Asian dishes

TYPE: Dark lager
TASTE: Flavored with roasted barley or malt, it tastes rich, malty, and sweet.
SERVE WITH: Roast chicken or sausage dishes

ALES

TYPE: Pale ale
TASTE: Dry and slightly bitter, with traces of fruit
SERVE WITH: Roast beef, prime rib, or steak

TYPE: Brown ale
TASTE: This full-bodied, copper-colored ale is sweet and malty. Some brown ales have hints of fruit.
SERVE WITH: Flavorful red meats, wild game, or sausage

TYPE: Porter
TASTE: Made from roasted barley or barley malt, porters taste much like bittersweet chocolate.
SERVE WITH: Hearty soups and stews or meats with rich, brown sauces

TYPE: Stout
TASTE: Stout is the darkest, densest ale. It ranges from sweet and dry to extremely bitter (burnt-tasting) and has intense malt and caramel flavors.
SERVE WITH: Shellfish, hearty stews, or wild game

WINE

Wine is a rich, boundless topic. If you dream of being a sommelier, there are hundreds of books and courses to choose from and millions of bottles to taste. For entertaining purposes, it isn't necessary to get bogged down in flowery adjectives or spend a lot of money. All you need are the basics on different wines and the foods they complement. For extra guidance, pick up a copy of Wine with Food, *by Joanna Simon; or* The Wine Lover's Cookbook, *by Sid Goldstein. It also helps to cultivate a relationship with a local wine merchant. He or she will get to know your tastes and give you specific tips and suggestions. Overwhelmed? Not to worry. Simply refer to this guide to the major wine grape varieties when planning what to serve at a luncheon or dinner party.*

WHITES

GRAPE: Chardonnay
TASTE: From crisp and mineral-y with citrus notes to full-bodied and opulent with flavors of butterscotch, vanilla, hazelnut, and toasty oak
SERVE WITH: Oysters, poached salmon, grilled tuna, seafood risotto, seared scallops, fish in a light butter or wine sauce, or roast chicken
BEST SOURCES: California (Napa Valley, Sonoma, and Central Coast), France (Burgundy)

GRAPE: Gewürztraminer
TASTE: Spicy and floral, extravagantly aromatic with a pronounced flavor of lychee
SERVE WITH: Bold spicy dishes, such as Thai curries, Szechuan and Hunan cuisines, or Asian fusion dishes
BEST SOURCES: France (Alsace), Washington state

GRAPE: Pinot Grigio (known in Alsace as Pinot Gris)
TASTE: Fruity and light with hints of apple, peach, or pear, Pinot Grigio has a subtle taste, which makes it very easy to drink.
SERVE WITH: Shellfish, grilled fish, roasted chicken, or pork tenderloin. Also great with omelets or frittatas

BEST SOURCES: Italy (Alto Adige and Provincia di Pavia), France (Alsace)

GRAPE: Riesling
TASTE: Crisp and refreshing, with a floral perfume and notes of tart apple and citrus. Riesling can be dry (trocken) or have various levels of sweetness from kabinett up to trockenbeerenauslese, one of the great dessert wines of the world.
SERVE WITH: Hors d'oeuvres, white asparagus, smoked salmon and fish, especially trout, in a sauce. It's particularly good paired with Asian and fusion food. And it's a classic warm-weather wine.
BEST SOURCES: Germany (Mosel-Saar-Ruwer, Rheingau, Rheinhessen, and Pfalz), France (Alsace), Austria (Wachau, Kamptal and Kremstal)

GRAPE: Sauvignon Blanc
TASTE: Grassy, fruity, and herbal, with, in the best examples, a lovely mineral character
SERVE WITH: Raw shellfish, steamed mussels and clams, or grilled fish. The classic great match is with a chalky fresh goat cheese.
BEST SOURCES: France (Sancerre and Pouilly Fumé from the Loire Valley), New Zealand (Marlborough), South Africa (Stellenbosch)

REDS

GRAPE: Cabernet Sauvignon
TASTE: Can be concentrated and lush, with layers of flavors such as black currant, blackberry, cassis, tobacco, cedar, sometimes eucalyptus, and even chocolate or licorice. Tannins give the wines great aging potential.
SERVE WITH: Steaks, chops, roast beef, leg of lamb, burgers
BEST SOURCES: France (Bordeaux), California (Napa Valley), Western Australia (Margaret River), Italy (Tuscany)

GRAPE: Merlot
Predominantly used as one of the components of Bordeaux blends, merlot also makes a great wine on its own, reaching its zenith in Château Petrus in Pomerol, one of the few Bordeaux that is 100% merlot.
TASTE: Soft, fruity, and intense, with rich plum and dark berry flavors and a velvety texture
SERVE WITH: Merlot is delicious with roast leg of lamb, baby lamb chops, roast duck, or squab.
BEST SOURCES: France (Bordeaux), Italy (Tuscany and Umbria), California (Napa Valley)

GRAPE: Nebbiolo
TASTE: A black grape, indigenous to Piedmont, which makes incredibly long-lived wines with a beautiful ruby color and marvelous aromas of dark plums, rose petals, lavender, and espresso. The greatest Nebbiolo wines are Barbaresco and Barolo; those labeled Nebbiolo are less expensive and a good choice for everyday drinking.
SERVE WITH: Braised meats or roasted game
BEST SOURCES: Italy (Piedmont— Barbaresco and Barolo)

GRAPE: Pinot Noir
TASTE: Marvelous silky texture, restrained fruit, and a seductive earthiness. May be the most nuanced of all the red varietals. At its best, it's magic. But there is a wide range in quality and price.
SERVE WITH: Boeuf bourguignon and other beef stews, prime rib and côte de boeuf, roasted veal, and lamb, or seafood such as salmon. Pinot Noir is one of the more versatile reds, beautiful with a wide range of foods, but too delicate for strong or spicy flavors.
BEST SOURCES: France (Burgundy), California (Russian River Valley, Carneros, and Central Coast), Oregon (Willamette Valley)

GRAPE: Syrah (known in Australia as Shiraz)
TASTE: Full-bodied with a firm acidity, flavors of wild herbs, black pepper, and dark cherries and plums, woven with intoxicating hints of Asian spices
SERVE WITH: Roasted and grilled beef and sausages, lamb, game, especially feathered game, even organ meats such as kidney and liver. Syrah is one of the main components in blends that make up the majority of Rhône wines, the most famous being Côte-Rôtie, Hermitage, Crozes-Hermitage, Cornas, Gigondas, and Châteauneuf-du-Pape.
BEST SOURCES: France (Rhône Valley), Southern Australia (Barossa Valley, Clare Valley, and McLaren Vale), California (Central Coast)

GRAPE: Sangiovese
TASTE: Dry red with overtones of dried cherries, tobacco, and spice
SERVE WITH: Cured meats such as salami and prosciutto, aged sheep's milk cheese, roast pork, grilled chops, or pastas with meat ragus
BEST SOURCES: Italy (Tuscany for Chianti Classico and Brunello di Montalcino and many Super Tuscans)

GRAPE: Tempranillo
TASTE: Made well, tempranillo can be lush and seamless. It has a sweet tone to the fruit and a dry finish. It tastes of red fruit, smoky wood, and wild herbs. Sometimes it has a perfume of cedar.
SERVE WITH: Cured sausages, serrano ham, roast suckling pig, roast lamb, or grilled meats
BEST SOURCES: Spain (Rioja and Ribera del Duero)

GRAPE: Zinfandel (known in Italy as Primitivo)
TASTE: They range in style from restrained and elegant to full-bodied, super extracted fruit bombs. Dark ruby-purple in color, the wines taste of cherries, dried plums, and spice.
SERVE WITH: Barbecued or smoked meats, ribs, burgers, cheeses, or wild boar
BEST SOURCES: California (Napa Valley and Sonoma)

WHICH WINES EXACTLY?

The following list of wine producers represents picks for best all-around value in taste, cost (between $8 and $45 per bottle), and general availability. Armed with this list, you'll never again wander aimlessly around the wine store.

WHITE

CHARDONNAY
Au Bon Climat (Central Coast, California); Brocard (Burgundy, France); Louis Jadot (Burgundy, France); Mt. Eden (Santa Cruz Mountains, California); Verget (Burgundy, France)

GEWÜRZTRAMINER
Hugel (Alsace, France); Trimbach (Alsace, France)

PINOT GRIGIO
Alois Lageder (Alto Adige, Italy); Livio Felluga (Friuli-Venezia Giulia, Italy); Venica (Friuli-Venezia Giulia, Italy)

RIESLING
Gunderloch (Rheinhessen, Germany); Hugel (Alsace, France); J.J. Prüm (Mosel-Saar-Ruwer, Germany)

SAUVIGNON BLANC
Babcock (Central Coast, California); Henri Bourgeois (Sancerre, France); Neil Ellis (Stellenbosch, South Africa); Villa Maria (Marlborough, New Zealand)

RED

CABERNET SAUVIGNON
Chateau Montelena (Napa Valley, California); Hess (Napa Valley, California); Marquis Philips (McLaren Vale, Australia); Penfolds (Barossa Valley, Australia)

MERLOT
Falesco Vitiano (Umbria, Italy); Havens (Napa Valley, California); Newton (Napa Valley, California)

NEBBIOLO
Produttori del Barbaresco (Piedmont, Italy)

PINOT NOIR
Castle Rock (Sonoma County, California); Chalone (Monterey, California); Louis Jadot (Burgundy, France); O'Reilly's (Willamette Valley, Oregon); Saintsbury (Napa Valley, California)

SANGIOVESE
Castello della Paneretta Chianti (Tuscany, Italy); Felsina Chianti Classico (Tuscany, Italy); Marchese Antinori Chianti Classico (Tuscany, Italy)

SYRAH AND SYRAH BLENDS
Guigal (Côtes du Rhône, France); Jaboulet (Rhône Valley, France); Ojai Vineyards (Central Coast, California); Qupe (Central Coast, California); La Vieille Ferme (Rhône Valley, France)

TEMPRANILLO
Emilio Moro (Ribera del Duero, Spain); Muga (Rioja, Spain); Pesquera (Ribera del Duero, Spain)

ZINFANDEL
Ravenswood (Sonoma County, California); Ridge (Sonoma County, California); Rosenblum (Sonoma County, California)

SPECIAL-OCCASION WINES

For a special occasion, these wines will have you digging deeper into your pockets ($25 and up) but they're unique.

WHITE

CHARDONNAY
Louis Jadot Corton-Charlemagne (Burgundy, France); Louis Latour Corton-Charlemagne (Burgundy, France); Neyers (Napa Valley, California); Ramey (Napa Valley, California)

RIESLING
F.X. Pichler (Wachau, Austria); Franz Hirtzberger (Wachau, Austria)

RED

CABERNET SAUVIGNON
Cos d'Estournel (Bordeaux, France); Joseph Phelps Insignia (Napa Valley, California); Pichon Lalande (Bordeaux, France); Ridge Monte Bello (Santa Cruz Mountains, California)

NEBBIOLO
Bruno Giacosa Barbaresco (Piedmont, Italy)

PINOT NOIR
Groffier Premier or Grand Cru (Burgundy, France); Dujac Premier or Grand Cru (Burgundy, France)

SHIRAZ
Clarendon Hills (McLaren Vale, Australia); Torbreck Descendant (Barossa Valley, Australia)

SYRAH
Guigal (Ampuis, France); Jamet (Côte-Rôtie, France)

SYRAH AND RHÔNE VARIETAL BLENDS
Beaucastel (Rhône Valley, France); Pegau (Châteauneuf du Pape, France)

TEMPRANILLO
Torre Muga (Rioja, Spain); Remírez de Ganuza (Rioja, Spain)

CHAMPAGNE

People tend to refer to all sparkling wines as Champagne, but only bubbly made from grapes grown in the Champagne region of France qualifies. Elsewhere, sparkling wine is called cava in Spain; it's known as spumante in Italy; and it's Sekt in Germany. In other countries that produce high-quality bubbly, such as the U.S., Australia, New Zealand, and South Africa, the name sparkling wine suffices. There are many excellent sparkling wines on the market, but Champagne is considered the gold standard because it's made using a centuries-old technique and aged for years (versus months in most other places). The cool climate and chalky soil of Champagne also produce highly acidic grapes, which are perfect for sparkling wine. Which ones to buy? Dom Pérignon, Taittinger Comtes de Champagne, and Krug Grande Cuvée are highly recommended for a special occasion. Good options for under $30 are California sparkling wines from Schramsberg, Roederer Estate, and Domaine Carneros.

THE FOOD

Food plays a starring role in every party, whether it's simple hors d'oeuvres with cocktails or a Thanksgiving feast. If the thought of cooking for large groups gives you pause, fear not. These strategies will help you plan what to cook, stock your kitchen and pantry for party success, and even choose the best cheese for a cheese plate, helping even the first-time cook stay cool in the kitchen.

PLAN YOUR MENU

Every party meal begins with a flash of inspiration—an inkling of what you're in the mood to eat and share with friends. These general rules will keep you covered no matter what foods you crave.

USE READILY FOUND FRESH INGREDIENTS. Nobody wants to eat pale, mealy tomatoes in December.

DECIDE HOW YOUR GUESTS WILL EAT. Will they eat at a table, or serve themselves from a buffet? Will they sit or stand in a larger space?

FOR A BUFFET, CONSIDER THE LOGISTICS. It's impossible to use a knife and fork while standing, so serve things like rice, cut up vegetables, and bite-size pasta versus steak. Avoid anything with bones. At a seated buffet, it's fine to serve roasted meat (which can be cooked and sliced in advance), but it is much harder to cook and replenish individual lamb chops.

BE REALISTIC. Unless you find cooking exciting or relaxing, don't feel pressured to wow guests with your culinary skills. The point of entertaining is to surround yourself with good friends and good things to eat. People are always thrilled to be invited to someone's home for a wonderful meal. They certainly don't—or shouldn't—care whether you peeled every shrimp or baked each cookie yourself.

OUTSOURCE. Buy frozen hors d'oeuvres such as mini quiches, pigs in blankets, and mushroom phyllo triangles, or order spring rolls or Chinese dumplings from a nearby restaurant. Desserts are also simple to buy, as are regional specialties like Maine lobster and North Carolina chopped pork (see The Resources, starting on page 180), which you can order a week or more in advance and flaunt as the mainstay of your party.

DON'T SERVE FISH. This doesn't apply to seafood pastas, paella, or bouillabaisse. And if you're a master with seafood, or fish is a huge part of your diet, ignore this point. Otherwise, take note: Typically, fish is fried, seared, or roasted, which must be done right before you serve it and requires meticulous timing.

PREPARATION

In theory, flash-fried oysters sound like an exciting and impressive appetizer, but in reality, they could cause more trouble than they're worth. When cooking for large groups, don't make any dish that requires great precision or last-minute maneuvers. Also, don't make too many different dishes. You'll spend much of the evening in the kitchen. (Larger quantities of fewer dishes is a better idea.) Every party guide in this book includes a specific timetable, but here are some general planning tips.

SHOP EARLY. Stock up on dry goods (paper towels, garbage bags, tableware, soda, alcohol, olive oil, condiments) as far in advance as possible. Buy groceries and ice one or two days in advance. Get a head start in the kitchen. The day or evening before an event, prepare as much of the food as possible. Wash and dry lettuce for a salad, snap off the ends of green beans, make dipping sauce, and bake dessert. Stews, casseroles, soups, and vegetable purées can also be prepared in advance. If you're really organized, make them a week before and freeze them.

EMBRACE YOUR OVEN. Braised meats like lamb shanks cook for several hours so you can start them early in the day. When they're done, all you have to do is remove the meat from the liquid, reduce the liquid into a flavorful sauce, and serve. Roast chicken and beef can "rest" for half an hour or more so you can time them correctly before things get last-minute crazy in the kitchen.

SAVE SIMPLE TASKS FOR LAST. It's unrealistic to think that you can have every detail in place when the doorbell rings. Certain steps, like dressing and tossing the salad, warming bread in the oven, slicing meat, and transferring food to serving platters, are perfectly appropriate once guests have arrived because they're contained, tidy, and easy to do while gabbing with friends. They may even want to help!

KITCHEN GEAR

If you already have a well-stocked kitchen, turn the page. If you don't have two pot lids to rub together, this checklist of essential equipment will get you cooking.

POTS AND PANS
8- and 10-inch high-quality nonstick skillets
3-cup saucepan with lid
2- and 3-quart saucepans with lids
3-quart sauté pan with lid
6- or 8-quart stockpot (shorter and squatter are more versatile)
7-quart Dutch oven that can go from the oven to the table
Roasting pan

KNIVES AND CHOPPING BOARDS
All-purpose 6-inch chef's knife
4-inch paring knife
Serrated bread knife
Kitchen scissors
Small, medium, and large plastic cutting boards

SPOONS, SPATULAS, AND MORE
2 long-handle wooden spoons, 1 solid and 1 slotted
Nonmetal spatula (for nonstick pans)
Long cooking fork
2 pairs of tongs, in varying lengths, with spring locks
2 whisks: a small flat whisk for emulsifying sauces and dressings and a medium-size balloon whisk for whipping cream and beating eggs

BAKING EQUIPMENT
Set of mixing bowls
Rolling pin
Extra-large nonstick mat for rolling pastry
2 metal baking pans: an 8- x 10-inch or 13- x 9-inch rectangle and an 8-inch or 9-inch square
1 or 2 metal muffin/cupcake pans
1 or 2 metal or glass pie pans
8-inch or 9-inch square or round cake pans
Set of rectangular glass baking dishes in different sizes
Cookie sheet (those with small edges are more versatile): 14- x 12-inch or 16- x 14-inch rectangle
Cooling rack

MISCELLANEOUS
Large measuring cup for liquids and a set of flat-bottom measuring cups for dry ingredients
A set of measuring spoons on a ring
Large colander
Can opener
Vegetable peeler
Salad spinner
Cheese grater/fruit zester
Instant-read meat thermometer
Ice-cream scoop
Timer

APPLIANCES
Food processor
Handheld or stand mixer
Immersion blender

THE CHEESE PLATE

A light spread can feel incomplete without cheese. It's perishable, of course, so you can't buy it in bulk and put it in a cupboard. But when stored properly—in the vegetable bin in the refrigerator, individually wrapped in wax paper or foil—cheese continues to age naturally and stays good for a few days (soft varieties) to a few weeks (hard ones). Buy it periodically; if you don't eat it with crackers, you can always grate it for omelets or

macaroni and cheese. When entertaining, serve three to five cheeses. When cheese isn't the main food being served, plan for 2 or 3 ounces per guest. The following descriptions will help you narrow your selection. And if you go to a gourmet or cheese shop, ask a salesperson for guidance—and samples. Take cheese out of the refrigerator half an hour before serving, to let its flavors unfold.

FRESH AND FRESH-RIPENED

WHAT THEY ARE: Mild, slightly tart fresh cheeses are uncooked and unripened, and range in texture from thick and creamy to moist and curdy. Fresh-ripened cheeses are slightly pungent, white in color, and have no rinds.

EXAMPLES: A few fresh cheeses are Italian mascarpone, ricotta, and mozzarella. Fresh-ripened cheeses include Bucheron and Montrachet.

SOFT-RIPENED; AKA BLOOMY RIND

WHAT IT IS: These rich, creamy cheeses have a high butterfat content and semisoft consistency. Molds are applied to their surfaces, causing them to ripen from the outside (Note: The moldy exteriors are edible).

EXAMPLES: Brie, Camembert, and double and triple creams such as Saint André

WASHED RIND

WHAT IT IS: These are the "stinky" cheeses. During the ripening process, they're brushed, rubbed, or submerged in a brine of salt water and wine, beer, or brandy, which promotes a moldy exterior and a pungent scent and flavor.

EXAMPLES: Pont l'Eveque, Munster, Livarot

SEMIHARD

WHAT IT IS: These mild cheeses, which are made from uncooked curds (milk solids), are ideal for snacking or dessert. Some of them, like Havarti, provolone, and Gouda, melt smoothly, which makes them great for cooking.

EXAMPLES: Asiago, Edam, Tomme de Savoie

HARD

WHAT IT IS: The curds that make up these hard, tangy cheeses are heated until they solidify and then pressed with weights into a firm consistency. Hard cheeses grow more pungent and crumbly with age.
EXAMPLES: Gruyère, Appenzeller, English-style Cheddar, Emmenthal, Jarlsberg, Manchego

BLUE-VEINED

WHAT IT IS: After being sprayed or injected with mold spores and aged in caves or cellars —under safe watch—bluish-green veins marble the interiors of these intensely flavored and pungent cheeses.
EXAMPLES: Gorgonzola, Roquefort, Stilton

THE PARTY-READY PANTRY

When friends drop by unexpectedly, it's important (and gracious) to offer them a drink and something to eat, regardless of what time they show up. The key to mastering such moments is to stock your pantry with a variety of high-quality dried, canned, and jarred goods that can be combined in many delicious ways or, if you have a bit of notice and can dash to the store, easily enhanced with fresh produce or meat to make a quick supper. The following items are available at most high-end grocery stores and gourmet shops, or from specialty food Web sites. (See The Resources, starting on page 180.) Keep them on your shelves and restock when necessary, and you can invite people over at the drop of a hat.

SNACKS

Beautiful presentation makes all the difference. Arrange snacks on an attractive cutting board, in a tapas tray with separate compartments, and in a few small, pretty bowls. Include any fresh veggies you may have like radishes, cherry tomatoes, or baby carrots. Buy a long, narrow dish to hold olives, and a beautiful cheese knife. Here's what to keep in the kitchen:

SMOKED OR SPICED NUTS

OIL-CURED BLACK AND GREEN OLIVES: To eat as is or as tapenade to spread on crackers or sliced French bread. (It's nice to keep jarred olives in the fridge too.) An opened jar lasts six months.

CRACKERS: Plain and flavored with herbs or pepper to serve with cheese, tapenade, pâté, salami, or other spreads. Crackers stay crisp and fresh for three to five days once the vacuum-packed seal is opened; toss any leftovers after that.

SLICED BAGUETTES: Freeze them in resealable freezer bags. To serve, defrost and toast.

CHEESE STRAWS: They stay fresh as long as crackers do.

DRIED FRUITS: Serve with cheese and nuts.

CHARCUTERIE: Cured salami can be stored in the refrigerator for up to three months.

CHEESES: See opposite page.

MUSTARDS: A strong, grainy one; a smooth Dijon; and something seasoned with jalapeño or honey to serve with salami or sliced ham on crackers or bread

DESSERTS

Around teatime and after dinner, people tend to crave something sweet. Keep a few of these goodies on hand, and be prepared to offer guests coffee and tea or an after-dinner drink too.

BISCOTTI

SCOTTISH SHORTBREAD

COOKIES

POUND CAKE: Keep in the freezer.

CHOCOLATE HAZELNUT SPREAD: Spread on pound cake.

BRANDIED CHERRIES: Serve on pound cake or with ice cream.

ICE CREAM, GELATO

CHOCOLATES AND CHOCOLATE-COVERED PRESERVED FRUIT

TOFFEE OR BRITTLE

HONEY-ROASTED NUTS

MEMBRILLO: A sweet quince paste that works well served on a cheese plate

GOURMET MARSHMALLOWS: For spontaneous s'mores

ARTISANAL HOT COCOA MIX

SWEET POPCORN

GOURMET DARK CHOCOLATE: Look for varieties packaged in pretty patterned paper for a special touch.

THE TABLE

At a luncheon or dinner party, the dining table is the center of the action, the place where guests and hosts convene for the main event. In other words, it better look good. That's not to say your table should be swathed in taffeta or anchored with an ice sculpture. It just needs to be pretty, inviting, not too busy, and a clear reflection of your personal style. The goal is to express your taste and the mood of the occasion. A general hint: Don't strive for perfection. Mix styles, colors, and materials until you strike the right balance between festive and functional.

TABLEWARE

Stock up on these multipurpose basics and, if you have room to store them, aim to have 12 to 16 place settings in your possession, which will accommodate most dinner parties.

DISHES

PLATES: A dinner plate measures nine to 10½ inches in diameter and works well as a main plate. A salad plate is eight inches in diameter and is suitable for salad, dessert, or cheese. A bread-and-butter plate is six inches or smaller in diameter.

BOWLS: Shallow soup bowls, which measure six to ten inches in diameter, are ideal for soup, pasta, stew, and chili.

FLATWARE

A BASIC PLACE SETTING: This consists of a dinner knife (you can substitute a steak knife if necessary), an all-purpose "place" spoon (smaller than a tablespoon and larger than a teaspoon), and a standard dinner fork, which is seven inches long.

OTHER KEY PIECES: These include salad forks, dessert utensils—forks and spoons (or dessert knives)—and bread-and-butter knives. If you serve fish often, you may want to invest in fish forks and knives too.

SERVING PIECES

DISHES: You'll probably need one large oval platter to serve a roast; one or two small oval platters to serve chops or other pieces of meat; one or two deep bowls to serve soft foods, such as mashed potatoes or creamed spinach; one or two shallow bowls to hold firm vegetables, fruit, or rolls; and one salad bowl. A very big, shallow bowl is also nice for serving unstructured entrées such as pasta, paella, or pot roast.

BOARDS: Modern entertaining, which strikes a balance between chic and casual, relies heavily on serving boards, both rustic and refined. Throughout these pages you'll see many innovative ways to use everything from simple wooden planks to polished slabs of marble to serve up sliders or an elegant cheese plate. Serving boards are easy to store, so stock up on interesting variations, maybe a color-dipped wooden board, a slate slab, and a rough-hewn antique cutting board.

UTENSILS: Essentially, you need spoons with both shallow and deep "bowls," slotted spoons to serve foods with juices that you want to drain, flat pieces (including pie servers for dessert) to pick up solid items, and a large fork to pierce dense foods. One or two of each is all you need.

OTHER SERVING ITEMS: Round out your tableware with pitchers for water, decanters for wine, salt and pepper shakers, sauce and gravy boats, and trays for carrying multiple dishes to the table.

GLASSWARE

WHAT YOU NEED: Each place setting requires at least two glasses: one water goblet, which holds at least six ounces of liquid when mostly filled, and one red or white wineglass, depending on what you're serving with the meal. (If you plan to serve both red and white, place both kinds of glasses on the table.)

GLASS SHAPES: White wineglasses are slightly narrower and straighter than red wineglasses in order to concentrate the flavor of white wine and slowly release its delicate bouquet. Red wineglasses are bigger and rounder to accommodate the more robust aroma and flavors of reds. To simplify matters, you can buy a large quantity of all-purpose, or Paris glasses, which work for both reds and whites.

LINENS

When choosing tablecloths, runners, place mats, and napkins, it's important to factor in the look of your dishes, glasses, and flatware, plus the décor (especially the color scheme) of your dining area. Start with a neutral tablecloth (white, ecru, or biscuit), then branch out with more vivid or patterned ones; the same applies to runners. Similarly, buy several sets of place mats and napkins in different hues and patterns, then combine sets in different ways to create different moods. Think about textures too: Smooth weaves go well with porcelain and china; coarser cloths better suit pottery and stoneware.

SETTING THE TABLE

Setting the table for a party shouldn't be intimidating. Though etiquette books offer a variety of ways to do it properly, depending on the level of formality of the meal and the food being served, there's one foolproof technique: Put down a plate. To the left of the plate, place forks (typically just salad and entrée forks) in the order in which guests will use them, with the first one farthest out. To the right, place knives and spoons, with knives closest to the plate and blades facing in. Again, order them so that you work your way inward as the meal progresses. Lay dessert utensils (fork and spoon, or fork and knife) horizontally across the top of the plate, spoon on top with its handle to the right. For fork and knife, the

fork is on top, handle to the left. You can also bring these out when you serve dessert. Arrange glasses on the upper right side of the place setting at a diagonal angle. Napkins go either on the plate or to the left of the forks.

FOR PEACE OF MIND: Set the table in the morning or even the night before a party. No one wants to deal with so many small components at the last minute. If you're serving a buffet, arrange the chafing dishes or platters and serving utensils early too, and for large buffets with many dishes, label each, using a Post-it, with the food you plan to put in it.

FOLDING NAPKINS

Keep things clean and modern by folding napkins into one of the following simple shapes. If you want to add a subtle adornment, tie a length of ribbon or colored twine around a folded or rolled napkin; you can slip a single flower or sprig of herbs underneath it.

CYLINDER: Start with a small rectangle or square. Fold it lengthwise into thirds and place it folded-side down on the center of the plate.

RECTANGLE: Fold the napkin into a small rectangle and place it to the left of the forks.

TRIANGLE: Start with a rectangle. Fold it over once or twice to make a square. Fold the square in half diagonally to form a triangle. Place it next to the forks, with the folded side closer to the plate.

SQUARE: Start with a rectangle. Fold the napkin over once or twice, depending on how big it is, then make a square that fits well on the center of the plate. Put it on the plate with the open side facing right.

SERVING STYLES

Once you've cooked and laid out your finest china, it's time to get the food from the kitchen to the table. Here are the four most standard serving methods:

FAMILY-STYLE

WHAT IT IS: Food is brought out in large serving dishes and placed on the table. Guests pass them around and serve themselves.

WHEN IT WORKS: At a casual or semiformal dinner, or when you have enough room on the table for the large bowls and platters

GETTING SECONDS: Food is passed around again as needed.

HELPFUL TIPS: To save yourself from last-minute scrambling, fill water glasses, set out plates of salad (or any other first course), and light candles before guests sit down.

PLATED

WHAT IT IS: Food is arranged on individual plates in the kitchen and brought out to guests.

WHEN IT WORKS: At a slightly formal dinner or when there's not enough room on your dining table for serving dishes

GETTING SECONDS: The host refills plates, or passes around serving platters, then returns them to the kitchen.

HELPFUL TIPS: Put bread, condiments, and beverages on the table. Guests can help themselves to those things.

SEATED BUFFET

WHAT IT IS: Food is laid out on a large table. Guests serve themselves and sit down to eat at a fully set table.

WHEN IT WORKS: When you have a large number of guests and enough tables and chairs to accommodate them. Seated buffets often take place at weddings and other large, formal parties, but are nice for smaller casual gatherings too.

GETTING SECONDS: Guests help themselves.

HELPFUL TIPS: Set up a buffet table near the kitchen and place it a few feet away from the wall if possible so guests can walk all the way around it. Use medium-size serving dishes and replenish food often—it will be fresher and look more attractive—and leave enough space between dishes for people to put down their plates if necessary. Stack plates on one or two ends of the table.

STANDING BUFFET

WHAT IT IS: Guests serve themselves from a buffet—place sets of silverware folded or rolled into napkins next to the stacks of plates—then stand or sit wherever they want, including sofas, stairs, and cushions on the floor.

WHEN IT WORKS: When you invite a big group of people for an informal meal. This works well at open house gatherings too.

GETTING SECONDS: Guests help themselves.

SEATING

There are all kinds of rules and regulations floating around about how to seat guests at a dinner party. Never put couples together! Boy, girl, boy, girl! While those do make sense in certain instances, they're really more of a starting point. The overall idea when seating people is to ensure fun, spirited conversation that engages all your guests throughout the meal.

EVENLY DISTRIBUTE YOUR LIVELIEST, most outgoing guests and mix old friends with new ones (don't group your closest chums together at one end of the table—they're likely to ignore everyone else). Alternating genders and dividing couples can lend an innocently flirty energy to a party, but neither is mandatory.

ONCE YOU DECIDE WHERE YOU WANT GUESTS TO SIT, put out place cards so you don't have to act like an air traffic controller at mealtime. Place cards make a party—and your guests—feel extra special. Formal, calligraphed cards are fine for black-tie dinners, but when entertaining in your home, take a lighter approach. Write names on colorful card stock, or stencil initials on strips of paper and wrap them around napkins. Use a gold or silver paint pen to write names on large leaves or baby pumpkins.

EXTRA HELP

When a guest list exceeds 15 or 20, depending on your space situation and anxiety level, it could be time to seek professional help. Renting equipment and hiring a bartender and a waiter (or two) may cost money, but it's guaranteed to save time, energy, and your sanity.

RENTALS: Renting plates, glassware, and flatware makes sense when entertaining a crowd, especially if guests will be spread out among several rooms; they're more likely to abandon several wineglasses in one night and to drop and break things. Party rental companies (that's how they're listed in the phone book) can determine the quantities you need based on your head count; be sure to arrange the details a few weeks in advance. They deliver everything the day of the party, and all you have to do is return things to their original crates for pickup the next morning. You can also rent larger items such as coatracks, tubs for wine and beer, and industrial-size trash cans for the kitchen. Prices vary across the country, but full supplies for a party of 25, including delivery and pickup, typically cost several hundred dollars.

HIRED HELP: A small hired staff will also ease your load considerably. A bartender keeps the drinks flowing during cocktail hour and can help serve food and clear plates at dinner. A waiter can set up the bar, heat and pass hors d'oeuvres, serve a meal, man a buffet, and clear and clean dishes. If you're unsure of how many waiters you'll need, call a catering company and describe your party. If you end up with more than one, assign them specific jobs. For example, one takes coats while the other heats the spinach pastry puffs; or one washes dishes while the other serves coffee and dessert. You can hire professionals from a catering company or enlist a few trustworthy college kids. Either way, plan to pay $20 to $30 per person per hour, for four to five hours, and don't forget to tip 15 to 20 percent in cash at the end of the night.

THE VIBE

Depending on the size and mood of your gathering and the amount of effort you're willing to put in, embellishments can range from understated to over-the-top. Regardless of your event, there are four elements you'll need to think about: furniture placement, lighting, music, and flowers.

PREPARATION

This begins long before the guests arrive. No wonder professional party planners think of each occasion as a theatrical event.

BEAUTIFY THE BATHROOM. Cleanliness is important, but so is easy access. Remove all personal belongings from the sink and counters (toothbrushes, contact lens cases, and shaving cream) and store them in the linen closet. Place an elegant bottle of liquid soap near the sink and a basket filled with dense, high-quality paper or cloth napkins nearby for drying hands. Place an extra roll of toilet paper in a visible spot, and light a candle or two so guests don't have to turn on a glaring, mood-killing overhead light.

PROTECT FURNITURE AND RUGS. For big parties, spray Scotchgard onto fabric upholstery and roll up valuable rugs. Always place coasters on surfaces that stain easily, such as wooden coffee tables and end tables.

DESIGNATE A CONVENIENT PLACE FOR COATS. If you're inviting more than 10 guests, it may be easiest to rent a coatrack and place it in your foyer. Otherwise, you can make room in a coat closet near the front door (be sure you have enough hangers) or pile coats on a bed. Just make sure to take everyone's coats—and offer to take purses too— the second guests walk in the door.

MAKE PLANS FOR PETS AND CHILDREN. Unless the event is very casual, keep pets away from the party area, and hire a babysitter to feed and entertain young children in a separate room. Many of the children's parents won't truly enjoy themselves unless they know their kids are well looked after and are having a good time. As a rule, it's nice to stock up on a few kid basics in advance, and just in case—a gallon of whole milk, some board games, a few balloons, crayons and drawing paper, or Frisbees and a soccer ball if the party is outdoors.

CLEAR THE WAY. The day before, remove all clutter from your party space and stash it in a designated room. That means stacks of magazines and mail, remote controls, laptops, big plants, kids toys, video games with long, tangled cords—anything that can get in the way of guests.

FLOWERS

There's no need to spend hundreds of dollars or fuss over the shade of every single petal. Simply go to a flower shop or market and pick out the prettiest, freshest-looking blooms. Then arrange them using these basic tips:

KEEP THINGS STREAMLINED. A dizzying combination of shapes and colors is inelegant. Stick with monochromatic flowers or a few shades in a similar palette. Shapes and textures should complement each other, never fight for attention.

USE CHIC VASES. The vessel should never upstage the flowers. Plain glass cylinders and bowls and silver mint julep cups are timeless, but other materials, like ceramic, wood, and tinted glass, can be just as sleek if they suit your party setting.

SPEND LESS WITHOUT SACRIFICING STYLE. If your budget is limited, buy a few large blooms and float them in low, clear bowls of water. If you're limited to grocery store bouquets, give them a quick makeover: Buy a few bunches and remove all greenery and baby's breath. Trim stems down to five or six inches. Group similar colors together in small vessels.

DON'T LIMIT YOURSELF TO FLOWERS. Fresh herbs, tropical greenery, branches of berries, boughs of holly, pinecones, and fruit all make lovely centerpieces.

PLACE FLOWERS IN ALL THE RIGHT SPOTS. Put arrangements where people will see them: in the entryway and on the bar, coffee table and buffet, and anywhere else guests will congregate. It's also nice to place a small arrangement, or even a few buds in a small glass, in the bathroom. Centerpieces belong, obviously, in the center of the dining table. You can place a large arrangement in the middle of the table or put several small ones in a line down the center. Make sure they don't block people's vision or take up too much surface area.

FURNITURE

When setting up a room for a cocktail party or open house, imagine a chic hotel lounge. Comfortable sofas and chairs are grouped in clusters to facilitate conversation.

REARRANGE FURNITURE. Create a few areas for people to gather, and make sure there's plenty of space for others to walk between them without tripping over a handbag or an extended leg.

SPREAD OUT SURFACE AREAS. Evenly distribute coffee and side tables so that everyone can grab food and set down a drink easily. Scatter large throw pillows for additional comfortable seating.

USE COMMON SENSE. The location of bars and buffets should encourage smooth traffic flow and discourage congestion. If you need more chairs and tables than you own, borrow them from a friend or rent them from a party supply company. If you entertain often, consider puchasing folding chairs and tables to store in a garage or attic until needed.

MUSIC

If you've ever seen a crowd evacuate a dance floor when "The Chicken Dance" starts playing, you understand the power of music at a party. It can truly make or break the mood, so spend some time planning what to play. The simplest approach is to let a streaming service do it all. But there are lots of other options. Here are some pointers:

START THE PROCESS A FEW WEEKS IN ADVANCE. Whenever you send out invitations is a good beginning point. Jot down artists or songs as you think of them. A few days before the event, make a party playlist for your digital music player. Once you have several hours' worth, you're set for the evening.

CUSTOMIZE THE SOUNDTRACK. A dinner might begin with light jazz and segue into Latin music. Brunch goes down smoothly with classical, folk, and bluegrass. A cocktail party could evolve from reggae and light funk to hip-hop and, if guests start dancing, disco. Getting together with a bunch of old friends? Bust out the greatest hits of the '70s, '80s, or '90s—whichever decade applies. And a luau wouldn't be complete without some tunes from Don Ho and the Beach Boys.

MIX IT UP. Rock, rap, jazz, country, soul, and even Broadway show tunes can coexist, as long as the songs flow smoothly into one another. Keep the vibe consistent so nothing sounds jarring. For ideas, check out the soundtrack, international music, and compilation sections on Spotify, or Surf Soundcloud for playlists and other eclectic mixes.

LIGHTING

Lighting is a crucial aspect in creating a sexy, inviting atmosphere, but it's easy to err on the side of cheesiness. Here's how to achieve the look you want:

REARRANGE LAMPS. You want your party space to be enveloped in an even glow. Make sure that bar and buffet areas have a little extra light so guests can serve themselves without spilling or breaking things.

BUY INEXPENSIVE DIMMERS. Found at hardware stores, dimmers attach to your lamps and light fixtures. Your space should be dark enough to feel special and intimate but light enough to see other people's faces—and the food.

INSTALL YELLOW OR PINK LIGHT BULBS. These colors cast warm, flattering light. Invest in a couple of uplights, which are shaped like canisters and sit on the floor. The best spots for them are behind the bar or buffet.

PLACE UNSCENTED VOTIVE CANDLES IN LOOSE CLUSTERS on all surface areas: tables, buffets, mantels, and windowsills. A few subtly scented candles keyed to the party's theme or season can be lovely—just place them away from food, fabric, plants, and books. White votives are classic and versatile, so buy them in bulk. Candles of varying heights can also create a warm, romantic ambiance.

KEEP SURROUNDING ROOMS DARK. This will enhance the jewel-box feel of the party area. If you don't want the other rooms to be pitch-dark, use low-wattage bulbs.

THE HOSTESS

You've cooked, decorated, and dimmed the lights. The Champagne's chilled, the stereo's cued, and guests are due in less than an hour. There's only one more detail to take care of—you! Leave yourself enough time and relish this opportunity to shine, slipping into a festive outfit and a celebratory mood. Take a deep breath! Here's how to make the most of playing host.

DRESS THE PART

After all the time and effort you've put into your party, you deserve to be the bright, shiny center of attention. Revel in the spotlight. Wear an outfit that's striking and glamorous, something with a wash of sparkle, an eye-popping color, or a dramatically dipping back. Make sure it's comfortable and flattering, and not too structured or confining. Have fun with accessories. Tuck a flower into your hair or slip on a pair of bejeweled Moroccan slippers. Bring out your most ornate chandelier earrings or a stack of gold bangles. Most important, give yourself time to get dressed, put on makeup, and do your hair. Do your hair and makeup earlier in the day, but save slipping into your dress until after you've done the heavy lifting, right before the party begins, to keep it looking fresh and to allow you more mobility as you prep. You can touch up hair and makeup then as well. If you can squeeze in a manicure and pedicure a day or two before, go for it. The less rushed you are, the more pulled together you will feel for the rest of the evening.

TAKE CARE OF YOUR GUESTS

This almost goes without saying, but there are a few key things a gracious hostess can do to put her guests at ease. The first is to stay near the front door while people are arriving, so nobody walks in and feels stranded. Recruit a friend to help and free yourself up to move about and tend to other party matters as needed. For large parties, hiring professional help to take control of the food, drink, and party logistics can also give you flexibility to focus on welcoming partygoers. Next, get a drink into guests' hands pronto by leading them straight to the bar or handing them a premade signature cocktail. Introduce disparate guests by mentioning a person, place, or interest they have in common so that they can continue conversation on their own. Rescue wallflowers by drawing them into a lively group. If there's a particularly shy or new guest who you worry might have difficulty conversing, consider asking another friendly guest ahead of time to keep an eye out for him or her. Try to spend the majority of a meal at the table, with friends. You'll be poised to restart stilted conversations, help guests get better acquainted, and, of course, bask in the fruits of your labor and the bliss of being surrounded by people you truly enjoy.

THE
PARTIES

——

Fun builds momentum—and when you're enjoying yourself, your guests will too. In the name of eliminating stress, we've eliminated the guesswork. In the following pages, you'll find all the specifics for hosting a range of parties, from a baby shower and an awards night party to a seasonal dinner and a cozy brunch, and more. Each chapter is broken down into an easy-to-follow format. The Scene covers invitations, décor, music, and any other mood-setting details. The Countdown spells out exactly what to do and when to do it. The Shortcut offers a slew of time-saving tips and ways to simplify party prep, just in case you decide on Saturday night to throw a Sunday morning brunch. But remember to use these guides in a way that suits you, whether you decide to re-create an event in detail, or simply use the chapters as inspiration.

DINNER PARTIES

—

BRAISED CHICKEN LEGS
WITH SPINACH & FENNEL
SALAD (PAGE 52); GLÜHWEIN
SANGRIA (PAGE 50)

COZY DINNER PARTY

When the days grow dark, it's time to gather good friends for a refined and rustic dinner of next-level comfort food. From a toasty baked Brie appetizer to a savory braised chicken main course to a nouveau take on spicy mulled wine, everything is served in a laid-back ambiance that encourages easy conversation and heartfelt connection. The focus is pure warmth, whether that means an actual fire laid in the grate or switching off the lights in favor of glowing candlelight.

BAKED BRIE WITH
CRANBERRY SAUCE (PAGE 52)

DINNER & DRINKS

Please join us for an evening of feasting by the fire

SATURDAY, JANUARY 6TH
AT 6:30 PM
THE WONGS' HOME
18 PIEDMONT LANE

PLEASE REPLY BY JANUARY 3RD

THE MENU

SIGNATURE DRINK: GLÜHWEIN SANGRIA

APPETIZER: BAKED BRIE WITH CRANBERRY SAUCE

MAIN DISH: BRAISED CHICKEN LEGS WITH SPINACH & FENNEL SALAD

DESSERT: INDIVIDUAL APPLE CROSTATAS

THE SCENE

INVITATION: A simple invitation with a woodgrain accent hints at the rustic nature of the evening.

DÉCOR: Serve the main dish family style, setting down an old-school enamel cooking pot right in the middle of the table. This meal is for sharing, and with succulent roasted chicken, braised winter vegetables, and rich porcini mushrooms, its one-pot star is a sensory delight, scenting the air and deliciously stoking the appetite. Cement tiles in traditional Moroccan patterns make great trivets, protecting your dining table from the heat while lending a worldly, graphic touch to the tablescape. In keeping with the evening's cozy mood, use a natural linen tablecloth or a folded plaid wool blanket as a runner and dark earthenware plates.

FLOWERS: Celebrate the moment with burnished winter leaves and clusters of bright berries gathered into small, rustically glazed ceramic vases with a natural, hand-hewn texture. Using the greenery at hand—what's in synch with the season and your spot—emphasizes the relaxed hominess of the evening. For another botanical touch, tie linen napkins with jute twine, tucking a sprig of berries into each.

MUSIC: Make a soothing playlist centered on the subtly sultry crooners of bygone times, such as Chet Baker, Billie Holiday, Sarah Vaughan, Lena Horne, Ella Fitzgerald, and Nina Simone. In the same vein, Django Reinhardt and Charlie Parker add a little jazziness to the mix. The overall goal is to underline the evening's cozy, homey feel without distracting from the table, or ever interrupting the great flow of conversation.

THE TAKE-HOME

No one will say no to a bite of chocolate at the end of the night. Break off big chunks of good, dark or milk chocolate and package them into a small paperboard box or an unbleached waxed sandwich bag tied with a linen, jute, or burlap ribbon and set out in a ceramic bowl next to the door. Alternately, serve roughly broken chunks of chocolate in a wooden bowl for guests to grab as they go.

THE COUNTDOWN

3 WEEKS: Send out invitations.

I WEEK: Stock up on candles. Pick up an enamelware pot, tile trivets, and ceramic vases. Buy all nonperishable items, including ingredients for the cocktail base.

5 DAYS: Put together your playlist. Package take-home gifts for guests.

2 DAYS: Shop for fresh ingredients, including those for the floral arrangements. Prep leaves and berry clusters.

DAY BEFORE: Make the mulled wine and refrigerate overnight. Spice-rub the chicken and refrigerate. Boil the cranberry sauce for the baked Brie. Peel citrus twists for the cocktails.

6 HOURS: Make the crostata dough and the oat topping. Organize the bar.

4 HOURS: Prepare the chicken and vegetable dish; refrigerate.

90 MINUTES: Make the apple filling. Fill and bake the crostatas. Set the table.

I HOUR: Set out the chicken prior to braising it.

30 MINUTES: Bake the Brie.

15 MINUTES: Set out ice for the cocktails.

5 MINUTES: Start the music. Top the braised chicken with the salad.

AS GUESTS ARRIVE: Light all the candles. Lay out the appetizer.

THE SHORTCUT

FLICKERING LED FAUX-CANDLES have come a long way, with recent technological advances making them a reliable alternative when you don't want to worry over wicks.

GATHER NATURAL FOLIAGE from the ground with time to spare, and coat the leaves with clear acrylic craft spray. This preserving trick keeps leaves from loosing their autumnal color or curling. Allow the foliage to dry for a day or two, then coat with the acrylic fixative on both sides, waiting 20 minutes in between.

REPLACE HOMEMADE DOUGH with puff pastry when making the apple crostatas. Similarly, gourmet granola makes a nice replacement for the oat topping.

PHONE A FRIEND the old-fashioned way. Unlike more formal occasions, a phoned invitation to a cozy dinner like this one is pitch-perfect and personal—not too casual, as an e-mail would be, and not too ceremonious, either.

THE POUR

This mulled wine brings together the warming spice of German Glühwein with the citrusy tang of Spanish sangria, served with a fresh sprig of mint. Be sure not to overheat either the spices or the wine when preparing the blend. The idea is to release the aromatic flavors of each element, without bringing out any bitterness.

GLÜHWEIN SANGRIA

SERVES 6
HANDS-ON 7 minutes
TOTAL 8 hours, 53 minutes (includes chilling)

½ cup sugar
½ cup water
Finely grated zest of I medium orange
2 star anise pods
2 (4-inch) cinnamon sticks
I teaspoon allspice berries
I teaspoon whole cloves
Fresh ginger, ½-inch slice, peeled
I bottle dry red wine, such as Carro 2012
½ cup aquavit
3 tablespoons fresh lemon juice
Crushed ice, for serving
Garnishes: lemon and orange twists, mint sprigs

I. In a medium nonreactive saucepan, combine the sugar, water, orange zest, anise, cinnamon, allspice, cloves, and ginger. Bring to a simmer over medium, stirring occasionally. Add the wine; bring to a simmer for 15 minutes. Remove from the heat and let cool 30 minutes. Strain and refrigerate overnight.
2. Stir the aquavit and lemon juice into the cooled wine. Pour the sangria into wineglasses filled with crushed ice; garnish with the citrus twists and mint.

GLÜHWEIN SANGRIA

THE RECIPES

BAKED BRIE WITH CRANBERRY SAUCE

SERVES 6
HANDS-ON 10 minutes
TOTAL 25 minutes

1   cup fresh or frozen cranberries
1   teaspoon orange zest, plus
    ¼ cup fresh juice (from 1 orange)
¼   cup packed light brown sugar
¼   teaspoon kosher salt
¼   teaspoon ground nutmeg
1   (8-ounce) Brie round
¼   cup chopped toasted pecans
Crackers

1. Preheat the oven to 350°F. Stir together the cranberries, orange zest, orange juice, brown sugar, salt, and nutmeg in a medium saucepan; bring to a boil over high. Reduce the heat to medium-low, and simmer, stirring often, until the cranberries have broken down and the mixture has thickened slightly, about 4 minutes. Remove from the heat.
2. Place the Brie on a rimmed baking sheet lined with parchment paper. Bake in the preheated oven until softened, 12 to 15 minutes. Transfer the Brie to a platter, and top with the cranberry sauce. Sprinkle with the toasted pecans, and serve immediately with the crackers.

BRAISED CHICKEN LEGS WITH SPINACH & FENNEL SALAD

SERVES 6
HANDS-ON 1 hour, 44 minutes
TOTAL 11 hours, 11 minutes (includes chilling)

BRAISED CHICKEN

6   whole chicken legs
1   tablespoon whole black peppercorns
1   tablespoon fennel seeds
1   tablespoon coriander seeds
¼   cup kosher salt
2   tablespoons fresh oregano leaves, coarsely chopped
Finely grated zest of 1 medium lemon
Finely grated zest of 1 medium orange
1   cup (1-ounce package) dried porcini mushrooms
3   tablespoons olive oil
4   ounces pancetta, diced into ¼-inch pieces
2   medium-sized red onions, diced into ¼-inch pieces
½   medium fennel bulb, cored and diced into ¼-inch pieces
1   celery stalk, diced into ¼-inch pieces
1   large carrot, peeled and diced into ¼-inch pieces
Table salt and black pepper
3   garlic cloves, minced
1   tablespoon tomato paste
1   tablespoon dried oregano
½   cup red wine vinegar
½   cup agave
½   cup white wine
3½   cups chicken broth
1   tablespoon unsalted butter
2   teaspoons fresh orange juice
1   tablespoon sliced fresh mint

SPINACH & FENNEL SALAD

10   ounces fresh baby spinach
1   medium fennel bulb, halved, cored, and thinly sliced
3   tablespoons Chardonnay vinegar
3   tablespoons olive oil, plus more for drizzling
1   tablespoon fresh lemon juice
Kosher salt and black pepper
5   ounces fresh goat cheese

1. MAKE THE BRAISED CHICKEN: Pat the chicken legs dry with paper towels; arrange in a glass 13- x 9-inch baking dish.
2. Combine the peppercorns, fennel seeds, and coriander seeds in a spice grinder; pulse until coarsely ground.
3. In a small bowl, mix the ground spices with the kosher salt, fresh oregano, and lemon and orange zests.
4. Season the chicken with the rub. Cover with plastic wrap, and refrigerate overnight.
5. The next day, allow the chicken to sit at room temperature for 30 minutes before cooking.
6. In a medium bowl, cover the dried porcini mushrooms with hot water; soak until softened, about 20 minutes. Remove the mushrooms and finely chop. Discard or save the soaking liquid for another use.
7. Preheat the oven to 300°F.
8. In a large stove-top-safe casserole pot, heat the olive oil over medium until shimmering. Sear the chicken in batches until golden brown, about 5 minutes per side. Transfer to a plate. Pour off the fat in the pot.
9. Add the chopped mushrooms, pancetta, and next 4 ingredients to the pot; season with table salt and pepper. Cook over medium, stirring occasionally, until most of the pancetta fat has been rendered and the vegetables are tender, 10 to 12 minutes. Add the minced garlic, tomato paste, and dried oregano. Cook, stirring, until the tomato paste is deep red, about 3 minutes.
10. Deglaze the pan with the red wine vinegar, agave, and white wine; cook

over medium-high, scraping up the brown bits from the bottom with a wooden spoon. Continue cooking until the liquid has reduced by two-thirds, about 10 minutes.

II. Return the chicken to the pot along with the juices and chicken broth. Carefully cover the surface of the braise with a piece of crumpled parchment paper cut to the diameter of the pot, and then put on the lid. Bring to a boil and then transfer to the oven to braise for 90 minutes, until the chicken is tender and easily pierced with a knife.

12. Take off the parchment paper; transfer the chicken legs to a platter with a slotted spoon. Cover with foil.

13. With the lid off, cook the braising liquid over medium-high until reduced by a third, about 10 minutes. Remove from the heat; stir in the butter, orange juice, and mint. Season with salt and pepper. Spoon the braising liquid over the chicken legs.

14. MAKE THE SALAD: In a large bowl, toss the baby spinach with next 4 ingredients. Season with kosher salt and pepper. Crumble the goat cheese over the salad and toss again. Serve immediately on top of the braised chicken, and drizzle with the olive oil.

INDIVIDUAL APPLE CROSTATAS

SERVES 6
HANDS-ON 50 minutes
TOTAL 3 hours, 15 minutes

DOUGH
I   cup plus I tablespoon all-purpose flour
3   tablespoons fine cornmeal, plus more for dusting
5   teaspoons granulated sugar
1¼   teaspoons kosher salt
9   tablespoons cold unsalted butter, cubed
3   tablespoons plus I teaspoon ice water

OAT TOPPING
¼   cup all-purpose flour
¼   cup old-fashioned uncooked oats
3   tablespoons light brown sugar, lightly packed
¼   teaspoon plus ⅛ teaspoon baking powder
¼   teaspoon plus ⅛ teaspoon kosher salt
3   tablespoons unsalted butter, melted and cooled slightly

APPLE FILLING
4   medium Granny Smith apples, peeled, cored, and thinly sliced
¼   cup plus 3 tablespoons sugar
I   tablespoon unsalted butter, melted and cooled
2   teaspoons all-purpose flour
2   teaspoons milk

I. MAKE THE DOUGH: In the bowl of an electric mixer fitted with the paddle attachment, blend the flour, cornmeal, sugar, and salt on low speed. Add half of the butter; mix on medium speed, about 5 minutes. Add the remaining butter; mix until dime-sized pieces of butter remain, about 3 minutes. On low speed, drizzle in the water and beat until the dough just comes together.

2. Remove the dough from the bowl. Pat into a 6-inch round and wrap in plastic wrap. Chill for 1 hour.

3. MEANWHILE, MAKE THE OAT TOPPING: Preheat the oven to 325°F.

4. Line a baking sheet with parchment paper. In a small bowl, whisk together the dry ingredients. Drizzle in the melted butter and stir to combine. Spread the mix on a baking sheet. Bake, stirring once,

until the topping is golden, about 20 minutes. Let cool.

5. MAKE THE APPLE FILLING: Put all the ingredients in a bowl; toss.

6. ASSEMBLE THE CROSTATAS: Line a baking sheet with parchment paper. Dust a work surface with cornmeal. Divide the chilled dough into 6 pieces; shape each into a 2-inch disk and cover with a damp towel. Roll out each disk into a 7-inch round, ⅛ inch thick. Transfer onto the baking sheet.

7. Top each round with 1 tablespoon of oat topping and a heaping ½ cup of apple filling, leaving a ½-inch border. Fold the edge of the dough over the apples. Top each crostata with another tablespoon of the topping. Refrigerate the crostatas for at least 20 minutes. Bake the crostatas at 325°F until golden brown, 50 to 55 minutes, rotating the baking sheet once halfway through. Cool slightly before serving.

SHAVED VEGETABLE SALAD
WITH PARMIGIANO-REGGIANO
& FRESH HERBS; BEET & AVOCADO
BRUSCHETTA (PAGE 60)

GREEN MARKET DINNER

Bountiful, colorful, and bursting with flavor, this elegant dinner is a feast for the senses. This scrumptious range of springtime dishes celebrates a new school of all-natural opulence—abundant in taste and deeply filling too. While the recipes are simple, and so is the décor, it's all about using what's fresh and beautiful in an optimal fashion, maximizing the potential of each element to create a gorgeous sense of plenty. Why not eat this way every night?

SEARED SALMON WITH
WHITE BEANS & SPINACH
(PAGE 62)

MADELINE AND JEAN HEBERT
INVITE YOU TO A

Spring Dinner

TO CELEBRATE THE SEASON

APRIL 22ND AT 7:00 PM
GOSFORD PARK #2

please reply

THE MENU

SIGNATURE DRINK: RETRO TOM COLLINS

APPETIZER: BEET & AVOCADO BRUSCHETTA

SOUP: ASPARAGUS SOUP WITH PARMESAN SHORTBREAD COINS

SALAD: SHAVED VEGETABLE SALAD WITH PARMIGIANO-REGGIANO & FRESH HERBS

MAIN DISH: SEARED SALMON WITH WHITE BEANS & SPINACH

DESSERT: PAVLOVA WITH BERRIES

THE SCENE

INVITATION: Play up this gathering's spritely garden-fresh inspirations with an invitation to match—delicately wreathed in leafy botanical designs that hint at a farm-to-table vibe while setting an elegant tone.

CENTERPIECE: Though the menu's focus is on lighter fare, the centerpiece you create should be exuberant, presenting nature at its most lavish and sumptuous. Pack the center of the table with a living display of all the freshest soft-petal blooms you can find—peonies and roses, in a pale mix of yellow, soft blush, and pink, as well as green hydrangea, lisianthus, scabiosa, and the occasional artichoke. If you have access to garden herbs, a variety of these work well in the mix. Tuck a floral frog into the bottom of a pretty serving bowl, crisscrossing the top of the vessel with a grid of floral tape to keep the blooms in place. Depending on the length of your table, you may want to repeat the look in smaller vessels—tiny crocks or silver cups—all along.

MENU: The trick to creating this soul-satisfying meal is to buy only the best ingredients—the nearest to just-picked as possible—and then to enhance, rather than to alter, their true flavors, preserving nature's delicious perfection. Your shopping efforts will pay off. The shaved vegetable salad will come together so easily, but it's worth taking the time to inspect and select each ingredient well. The same is true for the Pavlova's berries—choosing only the most flavorfully vibrant and plump berries will make all the difference.

THE TAKE-HOME

Tiny potted succulents bring a charming touch of color to each place setting and give guests a living memento by which to remember the evening. Alternately, use miniature pots of rosemary or thyme, herbs that are sure to be a welcome addition to any windowsill garden. Depending on your tableware, you might choose traditional terra-cotta pots or those in galvanized aluminum. The plants can also double as place card holders. Write each guest's name on the outside of a paper card and brief plant care instructions on the inside.

THE COUNTDOWN

3 WEEKS: Send out invitations.

2 WEEKS: Order miniature succulents or potted herbs. Source all the floral supplies needed to make the centerpiece.

I WEEK: Buy the liquor and all the nonperishable ingredients, including everything needed for the dressings and relish. Make the place cards.

2 DAYS: Shop for the fresh ingredients, including the salmon. Mix and bake the Parmesan coins; store in an airtight container.

I DAY: Make the centerpiece. Whip up the two dressings, for the appetizer and the salad, as well as the Olive-Lemon Relish (page 62).

NIGHT BEFORE: Lay the table. Bake the Pavlova base.

3 HOURS: Put together the soup. Toast the baguette rounds.

2 HOURS: Make the salmon dish; keep chilled.

I HOUR: Shave the vegetables for the salad and for the appetizer and store in the fridge. Rinse and trim the berries for the Pavlova.

30 MINUTES: Assemble the topping for the bruschetta, except for the avocado.

AS GUESTS ARRIVE: Slice the avocados; assemble the bruschetta. Warm the soup on the stove.

DURING APPETIZERS: Whip the cream for the Pavlova.

DURING MAIN COURSE: Assemble the Pavlova.

THE SHORTCUT

SUBSTITUTE PARMESAN COINS with baguette rounds dusted with grated Parmesan. Slice the baguette and lightly brush the rounds with olive oil. Then sprinkle with cheese and bake until golden brown.

PARE DOWN THE CENTERPIECE CONSIDERABLY, while still keeping the look whimsical. Instead of arranging flowers, go for a big bowl of artichokes placed in the center of the table, or gather every variety of kale—from

lacinato to curly red to Russian— as well as long sprigs of fresh herbs into an offbeat all-green bouquet, displayed in a straight-sided clear glass vase. You'll need variety and volume to pull this off, so do not skimp on the greens.

Either **FREEZE THE PAVLOVA BASE WELL IN ADVANCE,** or purchase individual premade meringue cups online. (If you opt to freeze a homemade base, allow three hours for it to thaw before preparing the dessert.)

THE POUR

With a wink at the original, this lightly sweet throwback has a delectable citrusy flavor. Long, tall glasses give the cocktail its classic look, while the maraschino cherry lends that perfect nostalgic touch.

RETRO TOM COLLINS

SERVES I
HANDS-ON 5 minutes
TOTAL 5 minutes

2   ounces gin
2   tablespoons fresh lemon juice
I   teaspoon superfine sugar
3   ounces club soda
I   maraschino cherry
I   orange slice

I. Combine the gin, lemon juice, and sugar in a cocktail shaker half-filled with ice cubes. Shake well.
2. Strain into a tall Collins glass filled with ice cubes. Add the club soda. Stir and garnish with the cherry and orange slice.

ASPARAGUS SOUP WITH
PARMESAN SHORTBREAD COINS
(PAGE 60)

THE RECIPES

BEET & AVOCADO BRUSCHETTA

SERVES 8
HANDS-ON 15 minutes
TOTAL 1 hour, 37 minutes

SALAD

4	medium-sized beets, washed, peeled, and diced
2	tablespoons olive oil
½	teaspoon table salt
½	teaspoon freshly ground black pepper
1	baguette, sliced into 16 pieces
½	fennel bulb
1	cup baby arugula
1	tablespoon chopped pistachios
2	avocados, cut into 16 wedges

DRESSING

1	orange, juiced
2	lemons, juiced
2	tablespoons olive oil
½	teaspoon ground cumin
½	teaspoon ground cardamom
1	tablespoon agave nectar
½	teaspoon kosher salt
¼	teaspoon black pepper

1. Preheat the oven to 400°F.
2. MAKE THE SALAD: Toss the beets with the oil, salt, and pepper. Roast at 400°F until tender, about 30 minutes, and cool.
3. Toast the bread slices in the oven.
4. MAKE THE DRESSING: Whisk together all the ingredients.
5. Using a mandoline or vegetable peeler, finely shave the fennel. Toss with the arugula, beets, and pistachios; dress lightly.
6. Place an avocado wedge on each bread slice; top with the salad.

ASPARAGUS SOUP WITH PARMESAN SHORTBREAD COINS

SERVES 8
HANDS-ON 1 hour
TOTAL 2 hours, 35 minutes (includes chilling and cooling)

2¼	cups all-purpose flour
8	ounces freshly grated Parmigiano-Reggiano cheese
1½	teaspoons dried thyme
1½	teaspoons grated lemon zest, plus more for garnish
2¼	teaspoons kosher salt
1⅛	cups unsalted butter, softened
3	large egg yolks
3	tablespoons unsalted butter
1½	medium onions, thinly sliced
2¼	pounds asparagus, cut into 1-inch pieces
1½	quarts low-sodium chicken broth
½	cup fresh tarragon leaves, plus more for garnish
1½	tablespoons flat-leaf parsley leaves
1⅛	cups heavy cream
¾	cup frozen baby peas, thawed
½	teaspoon freshly ground white pepper

1. Combine the flour, cheese, thyme, and 1½ teaspoons each of the lemon zest and salt in a stand mixer fitted with the paddle attachment. Add the softened butter and egg yolks and beat at medium speed until lightly moistened crumbs form. Gather the crumbs and knead to form a 2-inch-thick log. Wrap in plastic wrap and refrigerate until chilled, 30 minutes.
2. Preheat the oven to 325°F. Line 2 baking sheets with parchment paper. Slice the log into ¼-inch-thick slices and arrange on the baking sheets. Bake at 325°F until golden around the edges, about 20 minutes; let cool on the baking sheets.
3. Melt the 3 tablespoons butter in a large pot. Add the onions; cover and cook over medium, stirring, until softened, about 8 minutes. Add the asparagus; cook 2 minutes. Add the broth; simmer until the asparagus is tender, about 15 minutes.
4. Add the tarragon and parsley. Working in batches, puree the soup in a blender. Return the soup to the pot, add the cream and peas; rewarm. Season with the remaining ¾ teaspoon salt and the white pepper and garnish with tarragon leaves and zest, if desired. Serve with the Parmesan coins.

SHAVED VEGETABLE SALAD WITH PARMIGIANO-REGGIANO & FRESH HERBS

SERVES 8
HANDS-ON 42 minutes
TOTAL 42 minutes

DRESSING

2	garlic cloves, finely minced
2	tablespoons honey
½	cup fresh lemon juice
4	tablespoons Champagne vinegar, or white wine vinegar
1	cup Arbequina olive oil, or other fruity olive oil
2	teaspoons kosher salt
1	teaspoon freshly ground black pepper

SALAD

2	pounds mixed summer and pattypan squash, sliced into thin coins on a mandoline
2	pounds mixed radishes and beets, such as watermelon radishes and candy-cane beets, sliced into thin coins on a mandoline
2	shallots, sliced thin on a mandoline
¼	cup lemon zest

SHAVED VEGETABLE SALAD
WITH PARMIGIANO-REGGIANO
& FRESH HERBS

2 cups fresh herbs, such as thyme, basil (torn), and oregano

7 ounces (2 cups) Parmigiano-Reggiano cheese, finely grated on a Microplane

Espelette pepper (a French chile) or Aleppo pepper (Turkish and tangy) to taste

I. MAKE THE DRESSING: Process the garlic, honey, lemon juice, and vinegar in a blender. With the blender running, drizzle in the olive oil. Add 1 teaspoon of the salt and ½ teaspoon of the pepper; set aside.

2. MAKE THE SALAD: Combine the squash, radishes and beets, and shallots in a large bowl. Season with the remaining 1 teaspoon salt and ½ teaspoon pepper, and toss with the lemon vinaigrette dressing.

3. Add the lemon zest, herbs, cheese, and pepper. Serve immediately.

SEARED SALMON WITH WHITE BEANS & SPINACH

SERVES 8
HANDS-ON 40 minutes
TOTAL 40 minutes

SALMON

8   tablespoons olive oil
2   pounds fresh spinach, tough stems removed, leaves washed well and dried
2   (15-ounce) cans white beans, drained and rinsed
½   teaspoon kosher salt
½   teaspoon freshly ground black pepper
4   tablespoons grapeseed or canola oil
8   (5- to 6-ounce) skin-on salmon fillets
⅛   teaspoon fleur de sel, or any coarse salt

OLIVE-LEMON RELISH

1   cup chopped pitted picholine olives, or other green brine-cured olives
2   lemons, preferably Meyer, peeled, segmented, and chopped; juice reserved
4   tablespoons extra-virgin olive oil
4   tablespoons chopped fresh parsley
2   small shallots, finely chopped
1   teaspoon honey, plus more to taste
1   teaspoon white wine vinegar, preferably Chardonnay
½   teaspoon kosher salt, plus more to taste
½   teaspoon freshly ground black pepper, plus more to taste

1. MAKE THE SALMON: Heat 4 tablespoons of the olive oil in a large nonstick skillet on medium-high. Add the spinach; toss gently. Once wilted, pour out any excess liquid.

2. Lower the heat to medium-low. Add the beans and the remaining 4 tablespoons olive oil; heat about 5 minutes. Season with ¼ teaspoon each of the salt and pepper. Set aside.

3. Heat the grapeseed oil in another large skillet on medium-high. Once hot, add the salmon fillets, in batches, skin-side down. Cook without moving them until the skin is browned and crisp, 3 to 5 minutes. (If you try to lift the salmon too soon, the skin will stick to the pan.) Use a spatula to flip the fish over; cook for another 3 to 5 minutes, or more as desired. Season with the remaining ¼ teaspoon each salt and pepper.

4. MAKE THE OLIVE-LEMON RELISH: Toss together all the ingredients gently, including the reserved lemon juice in a large bowl. Taste and add more honey, salt, and pepper, if needed.

5. To serve, divide the beans and spinach among 8 plates. Place the salmon on top. Add a dollop of relish. Finish with a pinch of fleur de sel.

PAVLOVA WITH BERRIES

SERVES 8
HANDS-ON 25 minutes
TOTAL 2 hours, 30 minutes (includes cooling)

1   pound mixed fresh strawberries, blackberries, and blueberries
3   tablespoons lemon juice, plus 1 teaspoon lemon zest
¼   cup packed dark brown sugar
1   teaspoon ground cinnamon
⅛   teaspoon ground allspice
1   cup granulated sugar
2   teaspoons cornstarch
4   large egg whites, room temperature
¼   teaspoon cream of tartar
1   cup heavy cream
1   vanilla bean, scraped (seeds only)

1. Toss the berries with the lemon juice and zest in a medium bowl. Add the brown sugar, cinnamon, and allspice. Mix well and refrigerate.

2. Remove all the racks from the oven except the one closest to the top. Preheat the oven to 275°F.

3. Mix the sugar with the cornstarch in a medium bowl; set aside. Using the whisk attachment of a stand mixer, whisk the egg whites and cream of tartar at high speed for 8 to 10 minutes, until the egg whites hold their shape and the whisk leaves a path in the whites.

4. Switch to medium speed; add the sugar mixture tablespoon by tablespoon, waiting until each spoonful is incorporated before adding more. The meringue should be firm and glossy.

5. Spoon the meringue into a large round onto a parchment paper-lined baking sheet coated with cooking spray. Tidy up the edges of the round with a kitchen towel.

6. Place the sheet in the oven; bake at 275°F undisturbed for 45 minutes. Rotate and bake for another 20 minutes. The round should be crusty when (very gently) touched. If not, bake for another 10 to 15 minutes. Remove from the oven and let cool.

7. Combine the cream and vanilla seeds using the whisk attachment; beat until somewhat stiff.

8. Top the meringue with the whipped cream and the berry mix. Serve immediately.

GRILLED AVOCADO SALAD
WITH PICKLED RED ONIONS
(PAGE 71); CRISPY CORNMEAL
FRITTERS WITH MUSTARD-
LIME SAUCE (PAGE 72)

LATIN FUSION FEAST

From Santiago to Bogotá, Buenos Aires to Lima, and Havana to Mexico City, Latin American cuisine is known for its depth of flavor and glorious flair. Our savvy spread presents an all-modern take on a few of the classics of pan-Latin cuisine. As with all successful celebrations, here the well-loved standards are presented in an intriguing new way, and in a rustic atmosphere that lets the beauty of the food shine.

MIGUEL AND TOMÁS
INVITE YOU TO JOIN THEM FOR A

LATIN FUSION FEAST

DINNER + MOJITOS + MUSIC

FRIDAY, JUNE 8TH AT 7 PM
1162 REMBRANDT STREET

PLEASE REPLY BY JUNE 3RD

THE MENU

SIGNATURE DRINK: MOJITO COOLER

MAIN DISH: SHRIMP & CHORIZO KEBABS
WITH TOMATILLO-AVOCADO PUREE

SALAD: GRILLED AVOCADO SALAD
WITH PICKLED RED ONIONS

SIDE DISH: CRISPY CORNMEAL FRITTERS
WITH MUSTARD-LIME SAUCE

DESSERT: HORCHATA ICEBOX CAKE
WITH SPICED MANGOES & SWEETENED
WHIPPED CREAM

THE SCENE

MENU: When putting together a fusion meal, it's important to brush up on your food literacy. Smoky grilled kebabs—*pinchos*—are a favorite in almost every Latin country. Crisp corn fritters are cozy comfort food, whether the Colombian *regañonas* or Puerto Rico's *sorullitos de maíz*. Quick pickles—*escabeches*—known far and wide, are thought to have been introduced to Latin cuisine by the Spanish conquistadors. Horchata, the beloved sweet milky drink, varies from region to region but is widely known as "the drink of the gods." Avocado, at the core of this menu—and a key ingredient in so many Latin dishes—has been a staple since the times of the Aztecs, Mayas, and Incas.

DÉCOR: Highlight the brilliant colors of these dishes with a deep palette, incorporating elements of dark wood and indigo-dipped linen. Modest matte flatware conveys a tried-and-true authenticity, while minimal floral arrangements—even simple fern fronds—bring a liveliness to the table without distracting from the food.

MUSIC: In keeping with the subdued décor, you'll want to select music to match—sultry, vocal-based tracks that create a warm, sensuous ambiance. Start with mid-century Brazilian bossa nova (think João Gilberto, Tom Jobim, Vinicius de Moraes, and Elis Regina). Then blend in some of Cuba's classic Latin jazz (Tito Puente and Frank "Machito" Grillo). Liven things up with a little Merengue, originating in the Dominican Republic.

THE ACTIVITY

Lotería, a traditional Mexican game similar to bingo, is fun to play at dinner (the game can be purchased through Amazon.com). The images on the *tablas* (game boards) each have a corresponding riddle that can be found online and printed. Place a *tabla* at each place setting, and draw a card from the top of the deck. Using the riddles, describe to guests the card you have drawn. If they have on their *tabla* the image corresponding to your card, they mark it. For example, for the riddle *The street lamp of lovers*, players would mark *La Luna*, "The Moon." The first player to mark off a full row wins.

THE COUNTDOWN

3 WEEKS: Send out sunny invitations. Choose a colorful top to wear—maybe something embroidered—paired with dark-dyed jeans.

2 WEEKS: Order Lotería cards and skewers for the kebabs.

I WEEK: Stock the bar with Mojito fixings, minus the mint.

4 DAYS: Put together an upbeat Latin fusion playlist.

2 DAYS: Shop for all fresh grocery items and for simple greenery for the table.

DAY BEFORE: Pickle the onions. Bake and chill the cake. Make the fritters. Thinly slice the limes for the Mojito cocktail.

MORNING OF: Grill the tomatillos for the kebab sauce and the avocados for the salad. Make the Mustard-Lime Sauce (page 72) and the mango mixture. Buy fresh mint and destem.

3 HOURS: Squeeze lime juice for the bar and refrigerate.

2 HOURS: Puree the tomatillo sauce for the kebabs.

I HOUR: Marinate the shrimp. Skewer the kebabs and assemble the avocado salad.

45 MINUTES: Reheat the fritters. Toss together the Spiced Mangoes (page 72).

30 MINUTES: Whip the cream and store in the refrigerator.

I0 MINUTES: Start the music!

5 MINUTES: Set out ice, fresh mint, and lime slices at the bar.

DURING APPETIZER COURSE: Grill the kebabs.

DURING MAIN COURSE: Top the cake with the whipped cream and Spiced Mangoes.

THE POUR

How can a cocktail this simple be so beguiling? The storied Mojito is pure sweet-tart magic.

MOJITO COOLER

SERVES 4
HANDS-ON 5 minutes
TOTAL 5 minutes

²/₃   cup fresh mint
³/₄   cup white rum
¹/₂   cup fresh lime juice
I0   teaspoons agave nectar
I¹/₂   cups club soda
Lime slices, mint leaves

Muddle the mint in a pitcher. Stir in the rum, juice, and nectar. Strain the mixture, if desired, and add the club soda before serving. Serve over ice. Garnish with the lime slices and mint leaves, if desired.

THE SHORTCUT

NO TIME TO MUDDLE MINT? Leave it to the experts and buy an artisanal Mojito cocktail syrup.

INSTEAD OF CHOPPING FRESH MANGO to top your cake, go with frozen chunks that have been thawed and drained in advance.

WHEN YOU ARE UNSURE whether your avocados are ripe and ready, carefully peel back the nub of a stem cap with your finger. If it comes away easily, revealing a peek of bright underneath, the avocado is perfect. If there is a brown spot beneath the cap, likely this avocado is overripe.

MOJITO COOLER

SHRIMP & CHORIZO KEBABS WITH
TOMATILLO-AVOCADO PUREE

THE RECIPES

SHRIMP & CHORIZO KEBABS WITH TOMATILLO-AVOCADO PUREE

SERVES 6
HANDS-ON 25 minutes
TOTAL 1 hour, 25 minutes

1   pound raw medium shrimp, peeled and deveined
1/4   cup finely chopped fresh cilantro
2   tablespoons fresh lime juice (from 1 large lime)
2   garlic cloves, minced
1/4   cup extra-virgin olive oil
8   ounces semi-cured Spanish chorizo, cut into 1/2-inch-thick slices
5   ounces poblano chiles (about 2 poblanos), cut into 1/2-inch pieces
9   ounces red onion (about 1 large onion), cut into 1/2-inch pieces
12   (12-inch) skewers
1   teaspoon kosher salt
1/4   teaspoon black pepper
Tomatillo-Avocado Puree (recipe follows)

1. Toss the shrimp with the cilantro, lime juice, garlic, and 2 tablespoons of the oil. Let stand at room temperature 1 hour.
2. Preheat the grill to high (450° to 550°F). Thread the chorizo, chiles, onion, and shrimp alternately onto the skewers. Brush with the remaining 2 tablespoons oil; sprinkle with the salt and pepper. Grill, uncovered, just until the shrimp turn pink and the sausage and vegetables are charred, 4 to 6 minutes, turning once. Serve hot with the puree.

TOMATILLO-AVOCADO PUREE

MAKES about 3/4 cup
HANDS-ON 20 minutes
TOTAL 20 minutes

1 1/4   pounds fresh tomatillos, husks removed
1/4   cup extra-virgin olive oil
1 1/2   teaspoons kosher salt
3/4   teaspoon black pepper
1   ripe avocado, peeled and quartered
1/4   cup fresh lime juice (from 2 limes)
2   garlic cloves

1. Preheat the grill to high (450° to 550°F). Toss the tomatillos with 1 tablespoon of the oil and 1/2 teaspoon each of the salt and pepper. Grill, uncovered, turning occasionally, until blistered and charred, about 7 minutes. Cool 5 minutes.
2. Process the grilled tomatillos, avocado, lime juice, garlic, and the remaining 3 tablespoons oil, 1 teaspoon salt, and 1/4 teaspoon pepper in a food processor until smooth, 2 to 3 minutes.

GRILLED AVOCADO SALAD WITH PICKLED RED ONIONS

SERVES 6
HANDS-ON 15 minutes
TOTAL 20 minutes

3   ripe avocados, peeled and halved
3   tablespoons extra-virgin olive oil
3   tablespoons fresh lime juice (from 2 limes)
1 1/2   teaspoons kosher salt
1/2   teaspoon black pepper
12   ounces multicolored cherry tomatoes, halved (about 2 cups)
1/4   cup fresh cilantro leaves
1 1/2   ounces Cotija cheese, crumbled (about 1/3 cup)
1/2   cup Pickled Red Onions (recipe follows)

1. Preheat the grill to medium (350° to 400°F). Brush the avocado halves evenly with 1 tablespoon each of the oil and lime juice. Sprinkle evenly with 1 teaspoon of the salt and 1/4 teaspoon of the pepper. Grill, cut side down, uncovered, until the edges begin to char, 5 to 7 minutes. Remove from the grill; set aside.
2. Toss together the tomatoes, cilantro, and remaining 2 tablespoons each oil and lime juice, 1/2 teaspoon salt, and 1/4 teaspoon pepper in a medium bowl. Let stand 5 minutes. Place the avocado halves, cut side up, on a platter. Top evenly with the tomato mixture, Cotija, and Pickled Red Onions.

PICKLED RED ONIONS

MAKES about 1 cup
HANDS-ON 5 minutes
TOTAL 1 hour, 5 minutes

1   cup hot water
1/2   cup red wine vinegar
1   tablespoon granulated sugar
1 1/2   teaspoons kosher salt
1   red onion, thinly sliced

Stir together the hot water, vinegar, sugar, and salt until the sugar dissolves. Place the onion slices in a medium bowl; pour the vinegar mixture over the onions. Cover and let stand 1 hour or up to 24 hours. Drain, discarding the brine.

CRISPY CORNMEAL FRITTERS WITH MUSTARD-LIME SAUCE

SERVES 6
HANDS-ON 25 minutes
TOTAL 25 minutes

1¼ cups (about 5⅜ ounces) stone-ground coarse cornmeal
2 tablespoons chopped fresh flat-leaf parsley
2 tablespoons chopped fresh chives
2 teaspoons chopped fresh tarragon
1 teaspoon baking powder
1 teaspoon kosher salt
½ teaspoon black pepper
¾ cup whole milk
1 large egg, lightly beaten
½ pound cooked shrimp, finely chopped
1 large egg white
Canola oil
¼ cup chopped mixed herbs, such as parsley, chives, and tarragon
Mustard-Lime Sauce (recipe follows)

1. Stir together the cornmeal, parsley, chives, tarragon, baking powder, salt, and pepper in a bowl. Add the milk and egg; stir until well combined. Fold in the chopped shrimp. Beat the egg white with an electric mixer on high speed until soft peaks form; gently fold the egg white into the cornmeal mixture. Set aside.
2. Pour the oil to a depth of ¼ inch in a 10-inch cast-iron skillet. Heat over medium-high until hot. Carefully drop tablespoonfuls of the batter, in batches, into the hot oil; cook until golden brown, 2 to 3 minutes per side. Transfer to a wire rack on a paper towel-lined rimmed baking sheet to drain; keep warm in a 200°F oven until ready to serve. Sprinkle the fritters with the chopped herbs. Serve with the Mustard-Lime Sauce.

MUSTARD-LIME SAUCE

MAKES ¾ cup
HANDS-ON 5 minutes
TOTAL 5 minutes

½ cup mayonnaise
2 tablespoons Creole mustard
1½ tablespoons fresh lime juice (from 1 lime)
1 teaspoon honey
¼ teaspoon kosher salt
¼ teaspoon black pepper

Stir together all the ingredients in a small bowl.

HORCHATA ICEBOX CAKE WITH SPICED MANGOES & SWEETENED WHIPPED CREAM

SERVES 8
HANDS-ON 30 minutes
TOTAL 8 hours, 30 minutes (includes chilling)

1 cup heavy cream
8 large egg yolks
¾ cup granulated sugar
¾ cup (6 ounces) spiced rum
1 teaspoon vanilla extract
1 teaspoon ground cinnamon
24 cinnamon graham crackers (from 1 [14.4-ounce] box)
Spiced Mangoes (recipe follows)
Sweetened Whipped Cream (recipe follows)

1. Beat the cream with an electric mixer on high speed until stiff peaks form. Cover; chill until ready to use.
2. Pour water to a depth of 1 inch into a medium saucepan; bring to a simmer. Maintain a simmer. Whisk together the egg yolks, sugar, rum, vanilla, and cinnamon in a medium-size stainless steel bowl. Place the bowl over the saucepan of simmering water; cook, whisking constantly, until the egg mixture thickens, about 10 minutes, stopping to scrape the sides of the bowl. Remove from the heat; whisk until the mixture is cool, 5 minutes. Remove the whipped cream from the refrigerator. Gently fold the egg mixture into the whipped cream. Chill 30 minutes.
3. Place 8 graham crackers, breaking to fit as necessary, in a single layer in a 9-inch square pan. Spread 1⅓ cups of the egg–whipped cream mixture over the crackers. Repeat the layers twice. Cover and chill 8 to 24 hours.
4. Top the cake with the Spiced Mangoes and Sweetened Whipped Cream just before serving.

SPICED MANGOES

MAKES 3 cups
HANDS-ON 15 minutes
TOTAL 15 minutes

2 ripe mangoes, peeled and cut into ½-inch pieces
1 tablespoon granulated sugar
1 teaspoon olive oil
¼ teaspoon ancho chile powder

Toss together all the ingredients in a medium bowl.

SWEETENED WHIPPED CREAM

MAKES about 2 cups
HANDS-ON 5 minutes
TOTAL 5 minutes

1 cup heavy cream
1 teaspoon vanilla extract
¼ cup powdered sugar

Beat the cream and vanilla with an electric mixer on medium-high speed until foamy. Gradually add the powdered sugar, beating until soft peaks form.

HORCHATA ICEBOX CAKE
WITH SPICED MANGOES
& SWEETENED WHIPPED
CREAM

ROAST CHICKEN
WITH VEGETABLES
(PAGE 81)

HARVEST DINNER

Don't shrink from that autumnal chill in the air—embrace it! This flavorful fall menu celebrates the great American harvest, bringing together friends to share creative dishes that showcase seasonal farm-stand ingredients. The welcoming array includes an innovative appetizer made with pumpkin, sliced pear, and a crumble of blue cheese, a scrumptious shaved Brussels sprouts salad, and classic roasted chicken with potatoes and root vegetables. And what better way to end the evening than with an old-fashioned tart made with apple, pear, and cranberries?

ALIYAH & ANTHONY

INVITE YOU TO JOIN THEM FOR A

Harvest Dinner

COME FOR A CASUAL MEAL AT OUR PLACE
SATURDAY, OCTOBER 20TH
AT 6:00 PM
285 LISPENARD STREET, 2B

PLEASE RSVP BY OCTOBER 16TH

THE MENU

SIGNATURE DRINK: GINGER-LEMON HOT TODDIES

APPETIZER: PEAR & PUMPKIN TART

SALAD: SHAVED BRUSSELS SPROUTS SALAD

MAIN DISH: ROAST CHICKEN WITH VEGETABLES

DESSERT: APPLE, PEAR & CRANBERRY TART

THE SCENE

INVITATION: Summon guests to this delicious and vibrant affair with an invitation that boasts rich autumnal colors.

MENU: This menu celebrates a host of cool-weather fruits and vegetables—apples, cranberries, leeks, parsnips, pears, pomegranates, pumpkins, and more.

CENTERPIECE: Like a modern cornucopia, this centerpiece is bursting with vegetal glory and is made by filling a shallow oval planter with potting soil and planting it around the center with a smattering of succulents (echeverias is a nice choice). Next, nestle in kale leaves in different varieties like curly, lacinato, and red, as well as a range of herbs like rosemary and thyme. Then tuck in a few bunches of radishes in groups of three. Allow stray herb sprigs or kale leaves to tumble over the container's sides creating a gentle, natural look.

DÉCOR: This table's opulent appearance begins with its foundational fabrics in eggplant, plum, and cranberry and continues with gold flatware and white plates. Top each setting with a maple leaf–shaped sugar cookie, which can be purchased at the store or made at home with a cookie cutter and a simple dough recipe. Cinch the napkin and cookie together with a string tied in a bow, and voilà: an elegant treat awaits each guest! Scatter textured white and gold votive candles around the table to add a final cozy touch.

THE ACTIVITY

In ancient Celtic cultures, carved turnips, beets, and potatoes were thought to keep evil spirits away. But that was before European settlers encountered the New World's pumpkin. Invite guests to join in the grand harvest tradition by creating mini-pumpkin tea lights. On the top of each pumpkin, use a craft knife to trace a circle just larger than the bottom of the votive. Let guests hollow out their pumpkins and carve designs into the vegetables' sides. You can also provide acrylic paints and paint brushes for further décor. Once guests finish embellishing their pumpkins, each can slip in a tea light.

THE COUNTDOWN

3 WEEKS: Send out invitations.

2 WEEKS: Source the succulents for the centerpiece, mini pumpkins for the carving activity, and votive candles for the table and to use inside the carved pumpkins. Source the table linens and white and gold serving pieces.

I WEEK: Plant the succulents in the centerpiece. Buy liquor and all nonperishable items.

3 DAYS: Shop for fresh ingredients for the meal and for the centerpiece. Arrange the herbs and radishes in the centerpiece.

2 DAYS: Make the Apple, Pear & Cranberry Tart (page 81). Set up the pumpkin carving activity with a basket of knives and candles.

DAY BEFORE: Truss the chicken. Chop the accompanying vegetables. Juice the lemons for the hot toddy blend. Seed the pomegranate. Keep chilled.

MORNING OF: Cook the hot toddy blend and refrigerate.

5 HOURS: Bake the dessert tart, but do not top it. Bake the appetizer tart, but do not top with the arugula and cheese mixture.

3 HOURS: Shave the Brussels sprouts. Toast the walnuts. If refrigerated, bring the dessert tart to room temperature.

2 HOURS: Bake the chicken.

I HOUR: Set the table, including the centerpiece.

15 MINUTES: Rewarm the hot toddy mix, stirring in the rum and brandy. Arrange the chicken and vegetables on the serving platter.

5 MINUTES: Light the candles.

AS GUESTS ARRIVE: Dress the Brussels sprouts salad. Scatter the arugula and cheese mixture on the appetizer tart; cut it into pieces.

THE SHORTCUT

LEMON TWISTS can be made the night before and refrigerated. Either thinly slice a lemon, slitting each round carefully to remove the pulp and pith, or use a citrus twist peeler to create ribbons of peel and snip them into shorter lengths.

SAVE YOURSELF TWO STEPS by using refrigerated pie crust for the dessert—or doubling the recipe, making one for the party and one to freeze for later.

SKIP THE HOT TODDIES and choose a favorite, trusted wine, rather than risking an unknown.

THE POUR

Here's a modern way to make this centuries-old curative with a burst of bright ginger.

GINGER-LEMON HOT TODDIES

SERVES 8
HANDS-ON 13 minutes
TOTAL 4 hours, 13 minutes

5	cups water
I	cup fresh lemon juice
I	cup honey
3	tablespoons finely chopped crystallized ginger
½	(3-inch) piece peeled fresh ginger, cut into ¼-inch-thick slices
½	cup golden rum
½	cup brandy
	Lemon zest strips (optional)

I. Place the first 5 ingredients in a 3-quart electric slow cooker. Cover and cook on HIGH for 4 hours. Remove and discard the ginger slices. 2. Stir in the rum and brandy. Ladle the mixture into mugs, and garnish with the lemon zest, if desired.

PEAR & PUMPKIN TART (PAGE 80);
GINGER-LEMON HOT TODDIES

THE RECIPES

PEAR & PUMPKIN TART

SERVES 6 to 8
HANDS-ON 20 minutes
TOTAL 50 minutes

1	(17.3-ounce) package frozen puff pastry sheets, thawed
½	(3-pound) sugar pumpkin, peeled, seeded, and cut into ¼-inch-thick slices
1	firm Bartlett pear, cut into ¼-inch-thick slices
½	teaspoon kosher salt
¼	teaspoon freshly ground black pepper
2	teaspoons olive oil
2	cups loosely packed arugula leaves
¼	cup crumbled blue cheese
¼	cup fresh pomegranate seeds
1	teaspoon red wine vinegar

1. Preheat the oven to 425°F. Unfold the puff pastry sheets, and place side by side on a baking sheet, overlapping the short sides ½ inch. Press the seam to seal. Score a ½-inch border on all sides, using a knife. Do not cut through the pastry.
2. Toss together the pumpkin slices, next 3 ingredients, and 1 teaspoon of the olive oil in a large bowl. Spread the mixture in a single layer on the prepared pastry sheets, leaving a ½-inch border. Bake at 425°F until golden brown, 20 to 22 minutes. Cool on a wire rack 10 minutes.
3. Toss together the arugula, next 3 ingredients, and the remaining 1 teaspoon olive oil in a bowl. Add salt and pepper to taste. Sprinkle the mixture over the tart; cut and serve.

SHAVED BRUSSELS SPROUTS SALAD

SHAVED BRUSSELS SPROUTS SALAD

SERVES 6
HANDS-ON 15 minutes
TOTAL 15 minutes

1	pound Brussels sprouts
½	cup toasted walnuts
3	tablespoons finely grated pecorino Romano cheese
1	lemon
3	tablespoons extra-virgin olive oil
½	teaspoon kosher salt
½	teaspoon freshly ground black pepper

Using a mandoline, thinly slice the leaves of the Brussels sprouts into a medium bowl. Add the walnuts and cheese. Finely grate the lemon zest into the bowl; halve the lemon, and squeeze the juice into the bowl. Drizzle with the olive oil. Season with the kosher salt and black pepper, and toss to combine.

ROAST CHICKEN WITH VEGETABLES

SERVES 6
HANDS-ON 30 minutes
TOTAL 2 hours, 10 minutes

1   whole chicken (about 5 pounds)
1   lemon, halved
2   tablespoons unsalted butter, softened
Table salt and black pepper
2   leeks, dark green leaves trimmed, halved lengthwise, cut into 2-inch lengths
2   carrots, cut into 1-inch pieces
2   parsnips, cut into 1-inch pieces, thick ends halved
2   small white turnips, peeled and halved
6   small red potatoes, halved
2   shallots, halved
2   sprigs fresh thyme
2   tablespoons olive oil
3/4 cup low-sodium chicken broth

1. Preheat the oven to 475°F. Coat a large roasting pan with cooking spray. Trim the chicken of excess fat. Place the lemon halves inside the cavity. Truss or tie the legs with kitchen string; tuck the wing tips underneath the body. Set the chicken in the center of the roasting pan and rub all over with the butter. Season generously with the salt and pepper.
2. In a large bowl, toss the leeks, carrots, parsnips, turnips, potatoes, shallots, and thyme with the olive oil. Season with the salt and pepper. Arrange the vegetables around the chicken; pour in ½ cup of the chicken broth. Roast for 25 minutes, then reduce the oven temperature to 400°F. Cook until an instant-read meat thermometer inserted into the thigh reads 165°F, 50 to 60 minutes.
3. Transfer the chicken to a large platter, cover loosely with foil and let rest for 10 to 15 minutes. Before serving, remove any excess fat from the roasting pan, then place the pan, with the vegetables and pan juices, over medium-high. (If there are not enough pan juices, pour in the remaining ¼ cup chicken broth.) Cook, tossing the vegetables, until warmed through, shiny, and glazed, 3 to 5 minutes. Uncover the chicken, surround with the vegetables, and serve warm.

APPLE, PEAR & CRANBERRY TART

SERVES 8
HANDS-ON 35 minutes
TOTAL 4 hours, 10 minutes (includes dough chilling)

DOUGH
1¼ cups all-purpose flour, plus more for rolling
4   tablespoons cold unsalted butter, cut into small pieces
4   tablespoons vegetable shortening, chilled
¼   teaspoon table salt
2   tablespoons ice-cold water, plus more, if needed

TART
1   cup fresh cranberries
1   cup powdered sugar
1   large or 2 medium Golden Delicious apples, peeled, halved, cored, thinly sliced
1   large Bosc pear, peeled, halved, cored, thinly sliced
1   tablespoon unsalted butter, cut into small pieces

1. MAKE THE DOUGH: Process the flour, butter, shortening, and salt in a food processor several times until the mixture is crumbly. With the motor running, add 2 tablespoons of the ice-cold water and process just until the dough forms a ball. Add more water, 1 teaspoon at a time, if the dough is too dry. Press into a disk, wrap in plastic wrap, and refrigerate for at least 2 hours and up to 2 days before using.
2. MAKE THE TART: Process the berries and sugar in a food processor until finely chopped. Transfer to a wire-mesh strainer set over a bowl. Drain for at least 30 minutes, or up to 2 hours. Reserve the juices.
3. Preheat the oven to 425°F. Roll out the dough on a lightly floured surface into an 11-inch round. Press into a 9-inch tart pan with a removable bottom. Trim the edges of the dough. (You can prepare the dough to this point up to 2 hours ahead; refrigerate.) Line the dough with parchment paper; fill with pie weights. Bake until the crust is firm, about 10 minutes. Reduce the oven temperature to 375°F; remove the parchment paper and weights. Bake until the crust is lightly browned around the edges, about 7 minutes more. Cool for at least 10 minutes.
4. Spread the cranberry mixture over the tart crust (reserve the juices). Arrange the apples and pear in a circle over the berries; dot with the butter. Bake until the fruit has softened and the edges are golden brown, 45 to 50 minutes. Let cool.
5. Pour the reserved juices into a small saucepan. Bring to a simmer over medium-low. Cook until the syrup is reduced to 3 tablespoons, 5 to 10 minutes. Brush the tart with the glaze. Cool before serving.

HOLIDAY PARTIES

NEW YEAR'S EVE COCKTAILS

Good cheer goes glamorous! Dazzle your friends by ushering in the New Year exquisitely with an array of decadent treats set in a festively glimmering tablescape, glowing with touches of gold that illuminate the scene. The menu is designed to indulge guests with a bit of caviar here, a bite of chocolate there, and a range of bubbly beverages done every which way. Best of all, once the crowd arrives, your heavy hosting duties are over. You're free to flit and float your way into a fabulous New Year.

BUTTERMILK-CORN BLINI WITH CAVIAR; HERB TARTINES; LAMB MEATBALLS WITH ARUGULA PESTO (PAGE 90); FIZZY GINGER PUNCH (PAGE 89)

PLEASE JOIN US FOR A

New Year's Eve Cocktail

DECEMBER 31ST | 8:00 PM
THE HILLARDS' HOUSE
23 OAK ROAD

PLEASE REPLY BY DECEMBER 17TH
BLACK TIE

THE MENU

SIGNATURE DRINKS: MARQUISE PUNCH;
FIZZY GINGER PUNCH

HORS D'OEUVRES: BUTTERMILK-CORN
BLINI WITH CAVIAR; LAMB MEATBALLS
WITH ARUGULA PESTO; HERB TARTINES

DESSERT: MINI CHERRY CHEESECAKES
WITH OREO CRUST

THE SCENE

DÉCOR: Rather than taking the evening's metallic palette to the limit, a less-is-more approach works well here. A scattering of clever geometric candleholders and tree ornaments lends that perfect twinkle to the table, as do modish gold-topped cocktail picks, a straight-sided gold ice bucket, or candles that look like they've been dipped in molten metal. Go with gold-rimmed plates, or tumblers flecked with gold, rather than a gold-all-over option. Platters in ivory or cream as well as matte white pottery soften the look.

FLOWERS: Play up the gilded theme by lightly coating tall leafy branches with metallic gold spray paint. Magnolia leaves, smooth and thick, work especially well, as do sago palm fronds, if you want to bring in a whiff of the exotic. For a more subtly burnished look, instead of using paint, layer a dusting of metallic gold mica powder over a thin coating of glue.

MENU: The occasion comes only once a year, so lay your table with the good stuff—luxe little bites, including mini caviar-topped blini and slabs of dark and white chocolate. Display gold foil–wrapped chocolate balls in a bowl, or package them as a party favor. It's important to remember that on these momentous occasions, everyone craves the tried-and-true, like a platter of toasted tartines topped with savory herbs and pecorino Romano. Lamb balls with pesto are filling without being heavy. One-bite mini cherry cheesecakes are a nostalgic reverie.

THE ACTIVITY

Let guests join the King Midas fun by offering a range of metallic temporary tattoos. Alternately, your crowd might love dressing up in old-fashioned crowns and tiaras cut from embossed foil paper. (Search online for "Dresden" tiaras, in the old German style, or Dresden trim.) Or, see The Resources, starting on page 180, for suggestions for where to purchase Dresden-style tiaras as well as temporary tattoos.

THE COUNTDOWN

6 WEEKS: Send out invitations, and follow up with a friendly phone call if you haven't had an RSVP after 2 weeks.

3 WEEKS: Buy all tabletop items, including serving ware, punch bowls, cocktail picks, candles, and any needed tableware or barware. Zero in on an ivory-and-gold outfit for the evening.

2 WEEKS: Shop for sparkling wines and all bar staples, including ingredients for the two punch recipes. Spray paint the foliage.

2 DAYS: Bake the cheesecakes and refrigerate. Make the cherry sauce for the cheesecakes. Make the sugar syrup for the ginger punch. Start to stage the buffet, blocking out space for each item, including the two punches.

DAY BEFORE: Make the lamb balls and pesto sauce. Fry the blini and store overnight in the fridge.

3 HOURS: Put preprepared items—olives, nuts, etc.—in their serving vessels. Lay out the blini.

2 HOURS: Set out the floral arrangements. Make the tartines.

1 HOUR: Top the cheesecakes with the cherry sauce.

45 MINUTES: Get dressed!

20 MINUTES: Make the punches. Warm the blini, and top each with the crème fraîche and caviar.

5 MINUTES: Set out the last of the refrigerated items. Light the candles and start the music.

THE SHORTCUT

SKIP MAKING THE BLINI and go high-low instead, dressing up thick, ridged potato chips with a dollop of crème fraîche and caviar.

SPREADING OUT A WIDE SWATH OF CONFETTI in gold, rose gold, and white makes a magnificent table runner—and a dramatic statement if you don't have the time to sort out all the individual golden touches shown for this party.

ANTICIPATE A CROWD—you never know who will show up—

bolstering the menu with some no-stress additions: a plate of shaved prosciutto, cheese straws, mixed nuts, fresh shrimp and cocktail sauce, and a big bowl of spiced olives. Remember, most sparkling wines boast minerality and high acid, so they easily cut through rich dishes and make an especially good pairing with foods that are fermented or cured.

WHEN SERVING UP A SPARKLING WINE, pour like a pro, going for a steady stream down the center of the flute.

THE POUR

This cheerful Marquise Punch offers a super-fruity splash, with raspberry juice, pear, and citrus, while the new-wave Fizzy Ginger Punch (at right) is abuzz with fresh, gingery flavor.

MARQUISE PUNCH

SERVES 8
HANDS-ON 10 minutes
TOTAL 10 minutes

1	pint raspberries
1	(750-milliliter) bottle pear lambic beer or cider (try Lindemans framboise lambic)
1	(750-milliliter) bottle dry Prosecco
10	dashes of Angostura bitters
1	red d'Anjou pear, thinly sliced
1	medium-sized orange, sliced
1/4	cup simple syrup (see note for making simple syrup on page 160)
1/4	cup fresh lemon juice

Place the raspberries in a large bowl or pitcher; gently press with a spoon until the raspberries split. Add the lambic beer, Prosecco, and bitters. Stir in the pear slices, orange slices, simple syrup, and lemon juice. Serve in small ice-filled cups, making sure that each serving is allotted some of each type of fruit.

FIZZY GINGER PUNCH

SERVES 8
HANDS-ON 15 minutes
TOTAL 1 hour, 15 minutes (includes cooling)

1½ cups granulated sugar
¾ cup chopped peeled fresh ginger
¾ cup water
4 (2-inch) lemon zest strips, plus
   ⅓ cup fresh juice, chilled
1 star anise pod
1 (750-milliliter) bottle Champagne,
   chilled
1 cup brandy, chilled
2 medium-sized oranges, cut into
   rounds

1. Combine the sugar, ginger, water, lemon zest strips, and star anise pod in a small saucepan over high. Cook, stirring constantly, until the sugar dissolves, 2 to 3 minutes. Cool completely, about 1 hour; pour through a fine wire-mesh strainer, discarding the solids.
2. Place ½ cup of the sugar syrup mixture in a pitcher. Cover and chill the remaining simple syrup up to 2 weeks; reserve for another use. Add the Champagne, brandy, and lemon juice to the pitcher; stir gently. Garnish with the orange rounds.

THE RECIPES

BUTTERMILK-CORN BLINI WITH CAVIAR

SERVES 8
HANDS-ON 25 minutes
TOTAL 25 minutes

2/3 cup all-purpose flour
1/3 cup corn flour
1 teaspoon granulated sugar
1 teaspoon kosher salt
1/2 teaspoon baking powder
2/3 cup plus 2 tablespoons buttermilk
1 large egg
5 tablespoons unsalted butter, melted
1/4 cup crème fraîche
2 to 3 ounces osetra caviar (about 3 tablespoons)

1. Sift together the flours, sugar, salt, and baking powder in a medium bowl. Whisk together the buttermilk, egg, and 2 tablespoons of the melted butter in a small bowl until combined; fold into the flour mixture, stirring until just combined.
2. Heat a nonstick skillet over medium. Add 1 tablespoon of the butter, and swirl to coat. Add the batter, 1 tablespoon at a time, to form 7 cakes. Cook until bubbles form and the edges are golden brown, 2 to 3 minutes. Flip and cook until slightly firm, about 2 more minutes. Remove to a plate, and cover with a towel to keep warm. Repeat the process 2 more times with the remaining butter and batter.
3. Place the warm blini on a platter. Top each with a dollop of the crème fraîche and caviar.

LAMB MEATBALLS WITH ARUGULA PESTO

SERVES 8
HANDS-ON 40 minutes
TOTAL 46 minutes

ARUGULA PESTO

2 cups firmly packed arugula
1/2 cup firmly packed fresh flat-leaf parsley
1/2 cup olive oil
2 garlic cloves
1/4 cup grated Parmesan cheese
2 tablespoons water
1 teaspoon fresh lemon juice
1/2 teaspoon table salt
1/4 teaspoon black pepper

LAMB MEATBALLS

2 pounds ground lamb
1/2 cup golden raisins, chopped
1/2 teaspoon ground cinnamon
3 teaspoons kosher salt
1/2 teaspoon freshly ground black pepper
1 cup breadcrumbs
2 large eggs, beaten
1 medium bunch scallions (white and light green parts), sliced

1. MAKE THE ARUGULA PESTO:
Process the arugula, parsley, olive oil, garlic, Parmesan, water, lemon juice, salt, and pepper in a food processor until smooth. Set aside.
2. MAKE THE LAMB MEATBALLS:
Place an oven rack in the second-highest position and heat the broiler.
3. Combine the lamb, raisins, cinnamon, salt, pepper, bread-crumbs, eggs, and scallions in a large bowl.
4. Shape the mixture into golf ball–size meatballs and place on a large foil-lined baking sheet.
5. Broil, turning once, until cooked through, about 6 to 8 minutes total. Serve with the Arugula Pesto.

HERB TARTINES

SERVES 8
HANDS-ON 22 minutes
TOTAL 22 minutes

1 bunch fresh basil
1 bunch fresh chervil
2 sprigs fresh tarragon
4 ounces pecorino cheese
4 cups arugula
4 tablespoons olive oil
1 garlic clove
8 thin slices whole wheat or multigrain baguette
1/2 teaspoon freshly ground black pepper

1. Pick the leaves from the basil, chervil, and tarragon. Finely chop the basil and coarsely chop the chervil and tarragon. With a vegetable peeler, shave the cheese (or coarsely grate it). Toss the arugula, herbs, and pecorino with 2 tablespoons of the oil in a large bowl.
2. Combine the garlic with the remaining 2 tablespoons oil in a small bowl. Rub the garlic on the bread. Heat a nonstick skillet over medium; add 4 slices of the bread in a single layer. Toast on both sides until lightly browned. Repeat the process with the remaining 4 bread slices.
3. Divide the herb mixture among the toasts and season with pepper.

MINI CHERRY CHEESECAKES WITH OREO CRUST

SERVES 12
HANDS-ON 37 minutes
TOTAL 6 hours, 42 minutes (includes cooling)

- 12 Oreo cookies
- 3 tablespoons unsalted butter, melted
- 8 ounces cream cheese, softened
- 1/3 cup granulated sugar
- 2/3 cup whole milk ricotta cheese
- 1½ teaspoons vanilla extract
- 2 large eggs, lightly beaten
- 1 cup cherries, pitted and chopped
- 2 tablespoons bourbon
- 2 tablespoons honey
- 1/8 teaspoon ground cinnamon
- 12 fresh mint leaves (optional)

1. Preheat the oven to 350°F. Coat a 12-cup muffin tin with cooking spray.
2. Process the Oreos in a food processor until crumbly. Add the melted butter; pulse for 30 seconds to combine. Evenly divide the Oreo mixture between the muffin tins. Press the mixture firmly to create the crust. Bake at 350°F for 5 minutes.
3. Beat together the cream cheese and sugar using a handheld mixer until smooth. Add the ricotta, vanilla, and eggs; beat until smooth. Divide the mixture between the muffin tins. Bake at 350°F for 15 minutes until set. Remove from the oven and cool. Cover and refrigerate until ready to serve. Before serving, let stand at room temperature for 10 minutes.
4. Meanwhile, in a small saucepan, combine the cherries, bourbon, honey, and cinnamon. Bring to a simmer. Simmer over low 8 to 10 minutes until the mixture is syrupy; let cool to room temperature. Spoon the cherry sauce over each cheesecake. Garnish, if desired.

MINI CHERRY CHEESECAKES WITH OREO CRUST

FLOWER CUPCAKES
(PAGE 99)

MOTHER'S DAY TEA

This essentially feminine celebration—all in honor of Mom—never looked so fresh, because while throwing a proper tea in the grand tradition requires at least a hint of old-fashioned formality, that doesn't mean that it has to be a dull affair. Here, everything from the tablescape to the menu is updated, with pretty, modernist touches to usher in a new era. The menu centers on seasonal tea sandwiches, showcasing spring's favorites including cucumber, mint, peas, and asparagus.

CUCUMBER TEA SANDWICHES
WITH MINT-CHILE BUTTER;
PEA & RICOTTA TEA
SANDWICHES; PROSCIUTTO-
ASPARAGUS TEA SANDWICHES
(PAGE 98)

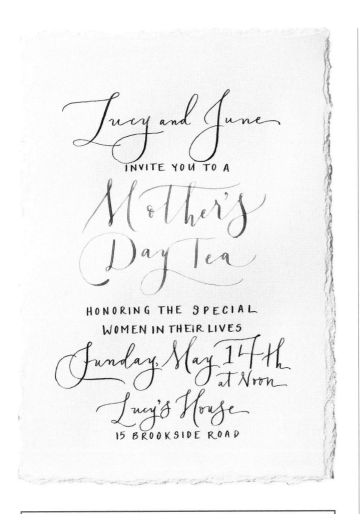

Lucy and June
INVITE YOU TO A
Mother's Day Tea
HONORING THE SPECIAL
WOMEN IN THEIR LIVES
Sunday, May 14th at Noon
Lucy's House
15 BROOKSIDE ROAD

THE MENU

SIGNATURE DRINK: VIRGIN BERRY SANGRIA

SANDWICHES: PEA & RICOTTA TEA SANDWICHES; CUCUMBER TEA SANDWICHES WITH MINT-CHILE BUTTER; PROSCIUTTO-ASPARAGUS TEA SANDWICHES

SIDE DISH: CHEDDAR & CHIVE SOUFFLÉS

DESSERT: FLOWER CUPCAKES

THE SCENE

INVITATION: The intimacy of this celebration calls for something special—a personal touch and an invitation that arrives by mail. If you want to go a step further, order professionally handwritten invitations, like this one from Brush & Nib Studio (see The Resources, starting on page 180), or hand-addressed envelopes. Otherwise, choose a hand-lettered look for your printed invitations—nothing too stuffy, but done in a font that twinkles with hand-drawn charm that all will adore.

DÉCOR: If the idea of throwing a tea makes you think of stiff chintz and flowery china, clear that too-traditional clutter and antique bric-a-brac from your mind. The look here is elegant and minimalist with a tone-on-tone palette centering on the subdued pastel color of your choice—palest pink, pure violet, or mint-y green. The trick is to choose only one color—or one for the tea table, and one for the dessert spread—and then to stick with it. Blush-toned tableware is paired with light pink linens, while lavender-gray dishes sit on a tablecloth in pale purple. All of these, however, mix well with European-style earthenware glazed in milky white.

FLOWERS: Here, too, you will want to accentuate your single color choice for the table, which will keep the arrangements from interrupting the quiet beauty of the tablescape. For a violet palette, go with sweet peas in a small cut-glass bud vase or dainty drinking glass. For a blush palette, choose lush garden roses either in a light pink or in creamy white to float in a small ceramic bowl.

THE TAKE-HOME

Even though Mom has finally mastered the art of the emoji, inspire written correspondence by giving each guest a packet of these old-fashioned, foil-stamped notecards. It's also sweet to get the ball rolling by sitting down after guests have gone to write each a letter of your own, reminiscing about the day, and reminding them why you treasure them.

THE COUNTDOWN

1 MONTH: Order hand-lettered envelopes. Choose stationery.

2 WEEKS: Send out invitations. Order macarons, petits fours, and glazed edible flowers, if not using fresh ones. Choose embossed cards to give as party favors.

1 WEEK: Shop for sangria supplies and all nonperishable items.

2 DAYS: Buy fresh vegetables, dairy ingredients, and fresh flowers.

DAY BEFORE: Take the cream cheese and butter out of the refrigerator to soften. Juice the limes for the cocktail. Make the cupcake frosting; keep chilled.

NIGHT BEFORE: Make the mint-chile butter. Make the cream spread for the prosciutto sandwiches. Blanch and slice the asparagus. Slice the cucumber; keep chilled.

MORNING OF: Remove the crusts from the sandwich bread. Prepare the sandwiches; chill. Bake and frost the cupcakes. Arrange the flowers.

4 HOURS: Set the table and arrange the dessert spread, except for the cupcakes.

2 HOURS: Lay out every ingredient for the soufflés. Set up the sangria station.

1 HOUR: Set out the sandwiches.

45 MINUTES: Begin assembling the soufflés.

5 MINUTES: Bring the cupcakes to the dessert table.

AS GUESTS ARRIVE: Set the soufflés into the oven to bake.

AFTERWARDS: Sit down to write a short note to each guest about why you're glad they came.

THE SHORTCUT

TAKE THE PRESSURE OFF by leaving dessert to America's most talented pastry chefs. Our pretty selection of macarons, petits fours, and tiny treats comes right to your doorstep (see The Resources, starting on page 180). Look for flavors that celebrate spring and complement your pastel palette.

SKIP THE SANGRIA. Offer guests a choice of green or black teas—two of each—remembering that in order to enhance the flavor, tea should never be made with water that's been left to simmer or with twice-boiled water. The quicker the water is heated, the better, because evaporation can raise the water's mineral content, resulting in bitterness. Preheat the teapot with hot water before brewing tea.

THE POUR

Light and airy, this bubbly and sweet spritzer is pure refreshment. And the sage leaf garnish lends a winning, jaunty touch. Add a dose of Mom's favorite alcohol for a spirited twist.

VIRGIN BERRY SANGRIA

SERVES 1
HANDS-ON 3 minutes
TOTAL 3 minutes

2	raspberries, plus more for garnish
2	ounces lemonade
1	ounce white cranberry juice
½	ounce fresh lime juice
2	ounces ginger ale
2	sage leaves, for garnish

1. In a cocktail shaker, muddle the berries. Add the lemonade and cranberry and lime juices. Add a handful of ice, and shake.
2. Strain the drink into an ice-filled glass; stir in the ginger ale. Top with the berries and sage.

THE RECIPES

PEA & RICOTTA TEA SANDWICHES

SERVES 12
HANDS-ON 15 minutes
TOTAL 53 minutes

12   slices white bread, crusts removed
3   cups fresh (or frozen) peas
2   garlic cloves
1/2 cup fresh ricotta cheese, plus more for serving
1/2 cup lightly packed fresh mint, plus small leaves for garnish
4   tablespoons finely grated Parmigiano-Reggiano cheese
4   tablespoons fresh lemon juice
2   tablespoons extra-virgin olive oil
Table salt and black pepper

1. Preheat the oven to 375°F.
2. Put the bread on two large baking sheets. Bake for 8 to 10 minutes, until crisp but not brown. Let cool.
3. Meanwhile, blanch the peas and garlic in boiling water until the peas are bright green and tender but not overcooked, 3 to 5 minutes. Drain well; transfer to a blender. Let cool.
4. Add the ricotta, mint, Parmigiano-Reggiano, lemon juice, and olive oil to the blender; process until nearly smooth. Season with the salt and pepper to taste.
5. Spread the puree on the toasts, then cut into quarters on the diagonal; transfer to a platter. Garnish with a dollop of ricotta and mint leaves.

CUCUMBER TEA SANDWICHES WITH MINT-CHILE BUTTER

SERVES 12
HANDS-ON 19 minutes
TOTAL 19 minutes

6   tablespoons butter, softened
3   tablespoons chopped fresh mint
1/4 teaspoon table salt
1   serrano chile, seeded and finely chopped
12   (1-ounce) slices white sandwich bread
1 1/2 cups thinly sliced English cucumber
1   tablespoon fresh lime juice

1. Combine the first 4 ingredients, stirring until well combined.
2. Trim the crusts from the bread; discard the crusts. Spread each bread slice with about 1½ teaspoons of the butter mixture. Place the cucumber in a small bowl, and drizzle with the lime juice; toss to coat. Arrange the cucumber slices in an even layer over the buttered sides of 6 bread slices; top with the remaining bread slices, buttered side down. Cut the sandwiches diagonally into quarters.

PROSCIUTTO-ASPARAGUS TEA SANDWICHES

SERVES 12
HANDS-ON 28 minutes
TOTAL 43 minutes

5   ounces cream cheese, softened
2   tablespoons fresh lemon juice
2   teaspoons grated white onion
1/4 teaspoon kosher salt
12   thin sandwich bread slices
2/3 pound blanched fresh asparagus
2 1/2 ounces thinly sliced prosciutto

1. Stir together the first 4 ingredients until well blended. Spread 1 tablespoon on each bread slice.
2. Cut the blanched fresh asparagus into thin ribbon-like strips, using a vegetable peeler. Divide the asparagus and prosciutto among the prepared bread slices. Gently press to adhere.
3. Cover with plastic wrap, and chill for 15 minutes to 12 hours. Trim the crusts from the chilled slices, and cut each slice into 2 triangles.

CHEDDAR & CHIVE SOUFFLÉS

SERVES 8
HANDS-ON 29 minutes
TOTAL 1 hour, 34 minutes (includes cooling)

4   tablespoons unsalted butter, plus more for greasing
Finely grated Parmigiano-Reggiano cheese, for dusting
1/3 cup all-purpose flour
1 1/2 cups whole milk
1/2 pound sharp white Cheddar cheese, shredded (2 cups)
6   large egg yolks
1/3 cup chopped chives
1/4 teaspoon cayenne pepper
Kosher salt
8   large egg whites

1. Preheat the oven to 375°F.
2. Butter 8 (10-ounce) ramekins and dust with the Parmigiano-Reggiano; tap out the excess. Put the ramekins on a large rimmed baking sheet.
3. In a medium saucepan, melt 4 tablespoons of the butter. Add the flour, and whisk over medium until thickened, about 1 minute. Gradually whisk in the milk and bring to a boil. Simmer over medium-low, whisking, until thickened and no floury taste remains, 5 to 7 minutes. Remove

CHEDDAR & CHIVE
SOUFFLÉS

from the heat, and stir in the Cheddar until melted, then stir in the egg yolks, chives, and cayenne until smooth. Scrape the mixture into a large bowl. Season with salt; let cool.

4. In another large bowl, beat the egg whites and a pinch of salt with an electric mixer at high speed until stiff peaks form. Whisk one-third of the whites into the cheese mixture, then gently fold in the remaining beaten whites until no streaks remain.

5. Spoon the mixture into the prepared ramekins. Bake for 25 to 30 minutes, until the soufflés are puffed and golden. Serve immediately.

FLOWER CUPCAKES

MAKES 48 mini cupcakes
HANDS-ON 35 minutes
TOTAL 1 hour, 32 minutes (includes cooling)

ANGEL FOOD CAKE
1   cup all-purpose soft-wheat flour
1/2 cup powdered sugar
1   cup granulated sugar

10   large egg whites
1   teaspoon cream of tartar
1/2 teaspoon table salt
1   teaspoon clear vanilla extract
2   teaspoons fresh lemon juice
1/2 teaspoon almond extract
Vegetable cooking spray

MASCARPONE FROSTING
1   cup whipping cream
12   ounces mascarpone cheese, softened
1   cup powdered sugar
1   teaspoon vanilla extract
1/8 teaspoon table salt

TOPPING
Edible flower blossom

1. Preheat the oven to 350°F.

2. MAKE THE ANGEL FOOD CAKE: Combine the flour and powdered sugar. Sift the mixture into a bowl; repeat the procedure. Whisk in 1/4 cup of the granulated sugar; set aside.

3. Beat the egg whites in a large bowl at high speed with an electric mixer

until foamy. Add the cream of tartar and salt, beating until soft peaks form. Gradually add the remaining 3/4 cup sugar, 2 tablespoons at a time, beating until stiff peaks form and the sugar dissolves. Add the vanilla, lemon juice, and almond extract, beating until blended. Sprinkle the flour mixture over the egg white mixture, 1/4 cup at a time, gently folding in after each addition.

4. Using 2 (24-cup) mini muffin pans lined with mini paper baking cups, coat with cooking spray and fill each cup two-thirds full. Bake for 10 minutes or until a wooden pick inserted in the center comes out clean. Cool in the pans on wire racks 10 minutes; remove from the pans to the wire racks, and cool completely.

5. MAKE THE FROSTING: Beat the whipping cream at high speed with an electric mixer until stiff peaks form. Beat the mascarpone, powdered sugar, vanilla, and salt in a large bowl at medium speed with a mixer until blended. Gently fold the whipped cream into the mascarpone mixture until blended.

6. Insert a metal piping tip into a large decorating bag, and fill with the frosting. Pipe a small circle of the frosting in the center of each cupcake. Top each frosting circle with an edible flower blossom. You may prefer to remove the flower before eating the cupcake.

TOMATO & CUCUMBER
FARRO SALAD; MINI
CHILI LOBSTER ROLLS (PAGE 106)

4TH OF JULY PICNIC

Flaunt your true colors this Fourth of July with stars
and stripes and sparks aplenty, throwing an outdoor bash
that's both sophisticated and fun. This sensational spread
brings together a just-right blend of tradition and taste.
Delectable mini-lobster rolls, a tomato and cucumber farro
salad, and a bedazzling layer cake add up to a menu that's
anything but run-of-the-mill. Best of all, so much can be
done in advance that come party-time all you'll have to do
is light the fuse.

TRUE-BLUE SUNDAES (PAGE 107)

PLEASE JOIN THE BURNABEES
FOR A

4th of July Picnic

FROM NOON–4PM
9732 WEST BEXHILL DRIVE
KENSINGTON, MARYLAND

RSVP

THE MENU

SIGNATURE DRINK: STAR-SPANGLED SMASH

SALAD: TOMATO & CUCUMBER FARRO SALAD

SANDWICH: MINI CHILI LOBSTER ROLLS

DESSERT: SPRINKLE LAYER CAKE; TRUE-BLUE SUNDAES

THE SCENE

INVITATION: Set the tone with a stylish but staid invitation that celebrates tradition in a crisp, straightforward way.

DÉCOR: The occasion calls for a generous splash of red, white, and blue, but it looks best in a simplified setting that's sleek and modern, with sparkling silver highlights. Deck the planks of a clean white-painted picnic table with masses of fresh red blooms, whether you choose a single variety or a mix of all sorts—ranunculus, anemones, and even perky gerbera daisies. Modern silver vases add a shining edge, gathered into clusters or lined up and down the center of the table. Starry cocktail stirrers bring a glimmer to the bar (their wooden sticks can be trimmed down ahead to suit cocktail glasses of any height). Blue or red splash-painted napkins lend an easy exuberance to the table, as do enamel splatterware serving bowls and platters, reminiscent of the ones you might find at an old-fashioned dry goods store.

MENU: Smarten up the snacks by serving potato chips in paper cones printed with graphic red and blue designs. Simply roll up each 9-inch paper square, securing it with double-stick tape at the bottom corner, and drop each into an ice-cream cone stand. You might also alternate chips with flavored popcorn—think savory and exciting, like chili-lime or sriracha-tamarind.

THE TAKE-HOME

At twilight's last gleaming, send guests off with a sweet parcel that celebrates the tricolors. Each artfully decorated, buttery shortbread—ordered directly from NYC's well-loved Eleni's Cookies (see The Resources, starting on page 180)—is embellished with a high-contrast splash, like fireworks bursting across the night sky. Slip one treat into a cellophane bag tied with red-and-white butcher's twine or ribbon, and line them up on a silver tray.

THE COUNTDOWN

I MONTH: Send out invitations.

3 WEEKS: Choose something white to wear.

2 WEEKS: Order cookies from Eleni's. Shop for music, tableware, vases, and napkins.

I WEEK: Package party-favor cookies for guests.

3 DAYS: Bake the star cookies for the sundaes.

2 DAYS: Bring home fresh flowers. Stir up a batch of cane syrup for the cocktails. (Simmer together 1 cup of cane sugar and 1 cup of water; store in the refrigerator.) Bake, frost, and decorate the cake. Store the finished cake in a cake container in the refrigerator.

DAY BEFORE: Shop for lobster, fresh berries, and mint. Make, but don't yet fill, the snack cones. Cook the farro; make the salad dressing.

6 HOURS: Arrange the flowers. Begin to decorate the space.

5 HOURS: Make the lobster-mayo mixture, and keep chilled. Prep and lay out the mini-buns, if they need preslicing.

3 HOURS: Remove the cake from the refrigerator, allowing it to come up to room temperature.

90 MINUTES: Get dressed!

30 MINUTES: Chop the tomatoes and cucumbers. Toss together the farro salad. Fill the snack cones.

DURING ARRIVALS: Assemble the lobster rolls.

DURING MAIN COURSE: Prepare the sundaes.

THE SHORTCUT

STAY HOME rather than decamping to a remote site, which requires much more work and forethought. Determine whether your own outdoor space—be it a backyard or patio—can work for an upscale picnic.

CAMOUFLAGE unattractive fencing with a string of linen pennants, alternating those in natural hues with others cut in denim or in ticking stripes, and all hung from butcher's string.

SUSPEND WHITE PAPER LANTERNS from the low branches of a tree to create a dreamy room-like atmosphere below. Use white or ivory paper pinwheels to edge a garden patch or lawn to delineate the festive space.

INDOOR-OUTDOOR RUGS make a great seating option for true picnicking as they are not as damp as blankets and are more resilient and tidy. Look for those in simple red or blue and white stripes.

THE POUR

Bright, fizzy, and full of ginger-y zing, this cocktail tastes like a sip of summer. When blending it together, shake hard enough to break up the berries, but not so much that the mint becomes bruised, which will make it taste bitter. (For an extra-amplified taste, try using Jamaican-style Reed's Extra Ginger Beer).

STAR-SPANGLED SMASH

SERVES 6 to 8
HANDS-ON 5 minutes
TOTAL 5 minutes

I³⁄₄ cups vodka
¹⁄₂ cup fresh lemon juice
¹⁄₂ cup cane syrup
I bunch fresh mint leaves
I pint fresh raspberries
I (12-ounce) bottle ginger beer

I. Stir together the vodka, lemon juice, syrup, mint leaves, and raspberries in a large pitcher.
2. Stir in the ginger beer just before serving. Serve in ice-filled glasses.

SPRINKLE LAYER CAKE (PAGE 107);
STAR-SPANGLED SMASH

THE RECIPES

TOMATO & CUCUMBER FARRO SALAD

SERVES 8
HANDS-ON 12 minutes
TOTAL 14 minutes

2   (8.5-ounce) packages precooked farro (such as Archer Farms)
3   tablespoons fresh lemon juice
2   tablespoons olive oil
2   teaspoons Dijon mustard
1   teaspoon table salt
1/2 teaspoon freshly ground black pepper
2   garlic cloves, minced
1   cup diced fresh tomato
1   cup diced cucumber
1/2 cup chopped fresh parsley leaves
1/2 cup chopped fresh mint
1/2 cup chopped scallions

1. Heat the farro according to the package directions.
2. Combine the lemon juice, olive oil, mustard, salt, pepper, and garlic in a medium bowl; stir with a whisk.
3. Add the cooked farro, tomato, cucumber, parsley, mint, and scallions to the lemon juice mixture; toss to coat.

MINI CHILI LOBSTER ROLLS

SERVES 10
HANDS-ON 20 minutes
TOTAL 2 hours, 20 minutes (includes chilling)

1   tablespoon canola oil
2   tablespoons finely chopped fresh ginger
2   tablespoons minced shallots
2   tablespoons mirin

MINI CHILI LOBSTER ROLLS

4   (1½-pound) lobsters, steamed, meat removed, and coarsely chopped
1   cup mayonnaise
3   tablespoons Sriracha chili sauce
2   tablespoons yuzu juice or lime juice
3/4 teaspoon kosher salt
1/4 teaspoon black pepper
1   cup finely chopped celery
4   scallions, green and white parts separated, each thinly sliced
2   tablespoons thinly sliced fresh mint
10 small potato rolls (such as Martin's Party Potato Rolls)

1. Heat the oil in a large skillet over medium-high until shimmering; add the ginger and shallots, and cook, stirring often, until the shallots are translucent and beginning to brown, about 3 minutes. Add the mirin, stirring to loosen the browned bits from the bottom of the skillet. Remove from the heat; add the lobster meat, stirring to coat.
2. Stir together the mayonnaise, Sriracha, yuzu juice, salt, and pepper in a medium bowl; add the lobster mixture, celery, white scallion slices, and mint, and stir. Cover and chill for 2 to 24 hours.
3. To create the mini buns, cut the rolls in half crosswise, and slice each piece halfway down lengthwise.
4. Fill the rolls with the lobster salad. Top with the green scallion slices and serve.

SPRINKLE LAYER CAKE

MAKES 1 (8-inch) layer cake
HANDS-ON 28 minutes
TOTAL 2 hours, 28 minutes

- ³/₄ cup red candy sprinkles
- ³/₄ cup navy blue candy sprinkles
- ³/₄ cup white candy sprinkles
- 2 (15.25-ounce) packages white cake mix
- 3 (12-ounce) containers white frosting

1. Preheat the oven to 350°F.
2. Lightly grease 3 (8-inch) round cake pans with cooking spray and line the bottoms with parchment paper.
3. Stir together the red, blue, and white sprinkles in a medium bowl.
4. In a large mixing bowl, make the cake batter according to the package directions. Stir in 1 cup of the sprinkle mixture and divide the batter evenly into the prepared cake pans.

5. Bake the cakes until a wooden pick inserted into the center comes out clean, about 34 minutes, rotating the pans front to back halfway through. Cool the cakes in the pans on wire racks for 10 minutes, remove them from the pans, and finish cooling on the wire racks until completely cool, about 1 hour.
6. Using a serrated knife, trim off the rounded tops (about ¼ inch) of each cake layer to make them flat. Discard the scraps.
7. Place 1 cake layer on the cake stand. Tuck four sheets of parchment paper under the cake, allowing the excess paper to hang over the edge of the cake stand (this will keep the surface clean while frosting). Use an offset spatula to frost the top with 1 cup of frosting. Repeat stacking and frosting the cake with the second and third layers. Use the remaining frosting to cover the sides of the cake and smooth the frosting all around, making it as flat as possible.
8. Center the cake stand on a rimmed baking sheet or inside a wide bowl. Using your hand, scoop the sprinkles and gently press them around the sides of the cake until the cake is completely covered.
9. Carefully remove the parchment paper. Serve immediately, or cover and store at room temperature for up to 3 days. The cake may also be covered and stored in the refrigerator for up to 1 week.

TRUE-BLUE SUNDAES

SERVES 8
HANDS-ON 1 hour
TOTAL 2 hours, 45 minutes

COOKIES
- ½ cup unsalted butter, softened
- ½ cup granulated sugar
- 1 large egg yolk
- ½ teaspoon vanilla extract
- ¼ teaspoon table salt
- 1¼ cups all-purpose flour, plus more for rolling

SUNDAES
- 2 pints vanilla ice cream
- 2 pints raspberry sorbet
- 1 pint blueberries

1. MAKE THE COOKIES: Use a stand mixer to beat the butter with the sugar at medium speed until fluffy, about 2 minutes. Beat in the egg yolk, vanilla, and salt, then add the flour at low speed.
2. Pat the dough into a disk and wrap in plastic wrap; refrigerate until chilled, about 30 minutes.
3. Preheat the oven to 350°F.
4. Line a baking sheet with parchment paper.
5. On a lightly floured surface, roll out a disk of dough ¼ inch thick. Using assorted star-shaped cookie cutters, stamp out the cookies as close together as possible; transfer to the baking sheet, 1 inch apart.
6. Bake the cookies in the center of the oven for 18 to 20 minutes or until lightly browned. Let cool slightly, then transfer the cookies to a rack to cool completely.
7. MAKE THE SUNDAES: Scoop ¼ cup each of the vanilla ice cream and raspberry sorbet into 8 bowls.
8. Sprinkle each with ¼ cup of the blueberries; top with 1 or 2 cookies.

SEASONED ROAST TURKEY
(PAGE 114)

THANKSGIVING DINNER

Celebrate America's best-beloved holiday with an inventive menu that riffs on all the old standbys in delicious new ways without overextending your time and patience. With nary a casserole in sight, this flavorful revival is easy to make and smartly updated. The turkey comes garnished with kumquats and fresh herbs. The carrots are spice-rubbed, barbecue style, while the sweet potatoes are done as an intriguing caramelized pavé. And last, but never least, comes pie—better yet, a creamy chocolate tart made with a crisp cocoa-pine nut crust. Don't panic. You've got this!

CORNBREAD WITH HONEY
BUTTER & SCALLIONS;
SEASONED ROAST TURKEY;
ROASTED GREEN BEANS & OKRA
WITH CARAMELIZED FISH SAUCE;
CARROTS WITH ESPRESSO,
DATES, SORGHUM & LIME
(PAGES 114-115)

MARIE AND PETER INVITE YOU TO

Thanksgiving Dinner

ON THANKSGIVING DAY AT SIX IN THE EVENING

THE FIERMAN RESIDENCE
7 VAN DEUSENVILLE ROAD | GREAT BARRINGTON

THE MENU

SIGNATURE DRINK: MAPLE OLD-FASHIONED

MAIN DISH: SEASONED ROAST TURKEY

SIDE DISHES: CARROTS WITH ESPRESSO, DATES, SORGHUM & LIME; CORNBREAD WITH HONEY BUTTER & SCALLIONS; ROASTED GREEN BEANS & OKRA WITH CARAMELIZED FISH SAUCE; SWEET POTATO PAVÉ

DESSERT: CHOCOLATE TART WITH PINE NUT CRUST

THE SCENE

FLOWERS: Break with the usual "autumnal" selections by turning to light, airy arrangements of creamy garden roses and small cheery chrysanthemums. Create a base for each arrangement using larger blooms in cream and white, or in the palest blush pinks and light greens, then add in a few stems in light plum or cranberry pink. (Though you may be tempted, remember—do not reach out for red, orange, or yellow.) These arrangements look best when the vessels—small rustic pitchers, for example—are not overpacked, so leave each stem a little breathing room.

DÉCOR: In a gently countrified palette ranging from silver-gray to muted indigo, choose soft linens, and simple tableware and ceramics with an artisanal, softly glazed look. Channel the Puritans of yore, and gravitate toward clean lines and simplicity over anything overtly embellished or baroque. For example, try a pared down saltcellar in hammered bronze and serving dishes, utensils, and candleholders in low-luster metals.

MENU: Out with the overrich and gooey and in with a fresh wave of tasteful American cuisine. This enlightened take on the traditional Thanksgiving menu celebrates freshness and innovation. However, when hosting the meal for your family, if there is one treasured dish that you know they can't live without, make it, and make it well (with no substitutions, alterations, or sarcasm). Chic is never as important as cherished.

THE ACTIVITY

It's too easy to forget what Thanksgiving is about. In the spirit of the day, set up a gratitude tree, offering guests the chance to express their thankfulness on its branches. Anchor pretty, bare branches in a vase, and using a maple leaf- and a feather-shaped template, cut out ivory, mid-blue, and maize gold paper cards. (Punch a hole at the top of each to pass a loop of string through.) Print with short prompts—"I wish . . ." or "I love . . ." or "I'm thankful for . . ."

THE COUNTDOWN

6 WEEKS: A Thanksgiving invitation requires plenty of advance. Send out a save the date.

1 MONTH: Mail out a detailed invitation.

2 WEEKS: Buy tabletop items.

1 WEEK: Stock up on spices, cocktail fixings, and hard-to-find ingredients like sorghum.

3 DAYS: Find pretty branches to use for the gratitude tree, and cut out paper cards shaped like leaves and feathers.

2 DAYS: Buy all fresh flowers, vegetables, and herbs, as well as dairy items and the turkey itself. Peel grapefruit twists for the cocktails; store in the refrigerator.

DAY BEFORE: Make the turkey spice blend. Make the chocolate tart and refrigerate.

NIGHT BEFORE: Whip up the Sorghum Sauce (page 114). Prep the turkey.

MORNING OF: Bake the cornbread. Roast the turkey. Arrange the flowers.

3 HOURS: Set the table. Bring the tart up to room temperature.

2 HOURS: Prepare the pavé. Cook the carrots.

45 MINUTES: Sauté the green beans and okra. Bake the pavé.

20 MINUTES: Set out ice for the cocktails. Rewarm the cornbread.

10 MINUTES: Light any candles that you might be using.

DURING THE MAIN COURSE: Top the tart with the whipped cream, pomegranate molasses, and pomegranate seeds.

THE SHORTCUT

TO EASILY CARVE thin slices of breast meat, gently cut the breasts from the turkey, placing them skin-side up on a board. Slice again from one narrow end to the other.

MAKE THE TART IN STAGES, baking and freezing the shell in advance. Or make the entire tart, thawing on Thanksgiving morning. You could even use a premade chocolate pie crust instead of starting from scratch.

IF YOUR TIME IS TIGHT, use a good cornbread mix, and top with the honey butter and scallions.

TEMPERING HELPS THE TURKEY COOK EVENLY, and keeps it from drying out, so remove the bird from the refrigerator 30 minutes to 1 hour before you actually cook it. That way the meat will be at room temperature all the way through before you begin roasting. But never thaw a frozen turkey on the counter. Bacteria will breed.

THE POUR

Some call the Old-Fashioned the original cocktail. Here, the iconic sweet-and-bitter classic is modernized with a delicious, woodsy maple flavor. Dark maple syrup is called for due to its complex and bold flavor.

MAPLE OLD-FASHIONED

SERVES 1
HANDS-ON 5 minutes
TOTAL 5 minutes

1½ ounces bourbon
1   grapefruit, juiced to equal 3 tablespoons fresh juice, plus 1 (2-inch) strip zest for garnish
1   tablespoon Grade A Dark with Robust Taste maple syrup
2   dashes of Angostura bitters

Combine the bourbon, grapefruit juice, maple syrup, and bitters in a rocks glass; stir. Add ice, and garnish with the grapefruit zest.

CARROTS WITH ESPRESSO,
DATES, SORGHUM & LIME
(PAGE II4)

THE RECIPES

SEASONED ROAST TURKEY

SERVES 12 to 14
HANDS-ON 29 minutes
TOTAL 3 hours, 44 minutes

I   (12- to 14-pound) fresh turkey
I   tablespoon table salt
2   teaspoons seasoned salt
I   teaspoon ground black pepper
I   teaspoon poultry seasoning
I   teaspoon garlic powder
I   teaspoon paprika
I   teaspoon cayenne pepper
I   teaspoon dried basil
½   teaspoon ground ginger
2   tablespoons butter, softened
I   cup water
Garnishes: kumquats, fresh sage,
     fresh rosemary

I. Preheat the oven to 325°F.
2. Remove the giblets and neck from the turkey. Rinse the turkey with cold water; pat dry. Place the turkey, breast side up, in a greased broiler pan. Combine the salt and next 8 ingredients. Using your fingers, carefully loosen the skin from the turkey at the neck area, working down to the breast and thigh area. Rub about one-third of the seasonings under the skin. Rub the skin with the softened butter; rub with the remaining seasonings. Tie the legs together with a heavy string, or tuck under the flap of skin. Lift the wing tips up and over the back; tuck under the turkey.
3. Add the water to the pan. Cover the turkey with aluminum foil. Bake at 325°F for 3 to 3½ hours or until a meat thermometer inserted into the meaty part of the thigh registers 165°F, uncovering the turkey after

2 hours. Transfer the turkey to a platter, discarding the pan drippings. Let the turkey stand 15 minutes before carving. Garnish, if desired.

CARROTS WITH ESPRESSO, DATES, SORGHUM & LIME

SERVES 6 to 8
HANDS-ON 40 minutes
TOTAL I hour, I0 minutes

ESPRESSO RUB
I   teaspoon ground espresso
½   teaspoon chili powder
½   teaspoon brown sugar
¼   teaspoon ground cumin
¼   teaspoon ground coriander
½   teaspoon table salt

CORNBREAD WITH HONEY BUTTER & SCALLIONS

SORGHUM SAUCE
¼   cup sorghum syrup
2   fresh sage leaves
2   tablespoons water
½   lime, juiced, plus zest for garnish
I   tablespoon unsalted butter
Table salt and black pepper

CARROTS
I6   large carrots, peeled
2   tablespoons extra-virgin olive oil
2   tablespoons unsalted butter
8   dates, chopped
Table salt and black pepper
2   tablespoons parsley leaves
I   tablespoon lime juice

I. MAKE THE ESPRESSO RUB:
Combine all the ingredients in a small bowl; set aside.

2. MAKE THE SORGHUM SAUCE: Combine the sorghum syrup, sage, and water in a small saucepan. Bring to a boil over medium-high; let cook, stirring occasionally, until reduced by almost half, 3 to 4 minutes.

3. Remove from the heat, then stir in the lime juice, butter, and salt and pepper to taste. Let stand 10 minutes; remove the sage.

4. MAKE THE CARROTS: Set a bowl of ice water aside. Bring a large pot of salted water to a boil over high. Add the carrots to the boiling water; cook until barely tender, 2 to 3 minutes.

5. Transfer the carrots to the ice bath; let stand 20 seconds. Remove to a clean towel, and dry.

6. Meanwhile, heat a large cast-iron skillet over medium. Add the olive oil and butter; let cook until the butter foams, about 1 minute. Cook the carrots in batches, adding half the carrots and half the espresso rub to the pan. Cook, turning the carrots once, until caramelized, about 6 to 8 minutes. (Do not turn the carrots too often or they will not caramelize.) Repeat with the remaining carrots and espresso rub.

7. Return the first batch of the carrots to the pan, then add the dates. Cook, stirring occasionally, until the dates soften, about 1 minute. Remove from the heat; season to taste with the salt and pepper. Transfer the carrots and dates to a plate; top with any pan juices. Spoon the Sorghum Sauce over the carrots; garnish with the zest.

8. Combine the parsley, lime juice, and a pinch of salt in a small bowl, then spoon over the carrots.

CORNBREAD WITH HONEY BUTTER & SCALLIONS

SERVES 8 to 10
HANDS-ON 20 minutes
TOTAL 45 minutes

CORNBREAD

1¼	cups cornmeal
1¼	cups all-purpose flour
2	tablespoons sugar
1½	teaspoons baking soda
½	teaspoon baking powder
1	teaspoon table salt
1	large egg
1¾	cups buttermilk
6	tablespoons unsalted butter, melted

TOPPING

2	tablespoons honey
1	scallion, thinly sliced

1. Preheat the oven to 350°F.

2. MAKE THE CORNBREAD: Whisk together the cornmeal, flour, sugar, baking soda, baking powder, and salt in a large bowl.

3. Whisk together the egg, buttermilk, and 4 tablespoons of the melted butter in a small bowl. Add the wet ingredients to the dry ingredients, stirring until just combined.

4. Heat a 10-inch cast-iron skillet on high with 1 tablespoon of the melted butter. Pour the batter into the pan. Transfer to the oven and bake until golden brown and a wooden pick inserted into the center comes out clean, 25 to 30 minutes.

5. MAKE THE TOPPING: Combine the honey and the remaining 1 tablespoon melted butter.

6. Remove the cornbread from the oven and immediately brush on the topping, then sprinkle with the scallions. Serve warm.

ROASTED GREEN BEANS & OKRA WITH CARAMELIZED FISH SAUCE

SERVES 6 to 8
HANDS-ON 30 minutes
TOTAL 50 minutes

1	pound okra, trimmed and sliced
1	pound green beans, trimmed
1	tablespoon rice wine vinegar
⅓	cup fish sauce
2	teaspoons brown sugar
1	garlic clove, peeled
5	cilantro sprigs, plus ¼ cup cilantro leaves, chopped, and more for garnish
2	teaspoons water
2	tablespoons lime juice

1. Preheat the oven to 450°F.

2. Combine the okra and beans on a baking sheet; roast for 20 minutes, until browned and just tender.

3. Combine the vinegar, fish sauce, sugar, garlic, and cilantro sprigs in a small saucepan with the water. Bring to a light simmer over high; cook until reduced by almost half, 6 to 8 minutes. Strain; set aside.

4. Three minutes before removing the vegetables from the oven, heat a large sauté pan on high until the pan is very hot. Remove the vegetables from the oven; pour the reserved sauce into pan (it should sizzle and come to a boil almost instantly); remove from the heat.

5. Add the vegetables to the pan; toss until coated. Stir in the chopped cilantro and lime juice. Top with more cilantro.

SWEET POTATO PAVÉ

SERVES 6 to 8
HANDS-ON 35 minutes
TOTAL 3 hours, 35 minutes (includes chilling and reheating)

3   shallots, thinly sliced
1/2 cup packed brown sugar
1/2 cup pecans, chopped, plus more
     for garnish
2   teaspoons fresh thyme leaves,
     picked, plus more for garnish
4   tablespoons extra-virgin olive oil
1 1/4 teaspoons table salt
1 1/4 teaspoons black pepper
7   sweet potatoes, unpeeled
     (optional), thinly sliced
Garnish: sugar (optional)

I. Preheat the oven to 350°F.
2. Cut 2 pieces of parchment paper to fit a 13- x 9-inch baking pan. Place 1 piece of parchment paper inside the pan; coat with cooking spray.
3. Combine the first 4 ingredients, 3 tablespoons of the oil, and 1 teaspoon each of the salt and pepper in a medium bowl. Layer one-sixth of the sweet potato slices on the bottom of the pan. Shingle them so they overlap completely. Top with about 1/4 cup of the shallot mixture.

4. Repeat with the remaining layers of sweet potatoes and shallot mixture, ending with sweet potatoes.
5. Brush with the remaining 1 tablespoon oil; season with the remaining 1/4 teaspoon each of the salt and pepper. Top with the remaining piece of the parchment paper; cover with another same-size pan. Add pressure to the pans while baking, perhaps with a cast-iron pan.
6. Bake for 50 to 60 minutes or until the sweet potatoes are tender. Cool completely with the pans still on top. Once cooled, transfer the pavé onto a cutting board; trim the jagged edges.
7. Cover tightly and store in the refrigerator until ready to heat and serve. Cut into even-size pieces, and reheat in a 350°F oven for 30 minutes.
8. While pavé is still warm, sprinkle with the sugar and caramelize with a torch, if desired. Garnish with a few thyme leaves and chopped pecans.

CHOCOLATE TART WITH PINE NUT CRUST

SERVES 8 to 10
HANDS-ON 30 minutes
TOTAL 6 hours, 22 minutes (includes chilling and cooling)

CRUST
I   cup all-purpose flour
I   cup blanched almond flour
1/2 cup unsweetened Dutch-process
     cocoa
1/2 cup pine nuts, finely ground
1/2 teaspoon fine sea salt
10   tablespoons unsalted butter,
     softened
3/4 cup granulated sugar

FILLING
I   cup unsalted butter
2 1/2 ounces 72% dark chocolate,
     chopped

I   cup packed light brown sugar
1 1/2 tablespoons unsweetened Dutch-
     process cocoa
1/2 teaspoon kosher salt
4   large eggs
Whipped cream, pomegranate
     molasses, and pomegranate seeds

I. MAKE THE CRUST: Whisk together the flour, almond flour, cocoa powder, ground pine nuts, and sea salt in a bowl.
2. In the bowl of an electric stand mixer using the paddle attachment, beat the butter and sugar at medium speed until fluffy, 2 minutes. Beat in the dry ingredients at low speed until a dough forms. Roll out the dough between 2 sheets of parchment paper to a 1/8-inch-thick round, about 12 inches in diameter. Refrigerate at least 2 hours or overnight.
3. Preheat oven to 350°F. Butter a fluted 10-inch removable-bottom tart pan, and press the dough into the bottom and up the side, trimming any overhang. Bake for about 25 minutes, until firm to the touch. Transfer the crust to a rack; let cool completely, about 1 hour. Reduce the oven temperature to 325°F.
4. MAKE THE FILLING: In a large heatproof bowl set over a saucepan of simmering water, melt the butter and chocolate, stirring occasionally, until smooth. Add the brown sugar, cocoa, and salt, whisking occasionally until the sugar is dissolved, about 3 minutes. Whisk in the eggs, 1 at a time, until the filling is shiny and smooth.
5. Pour the filling into the tart shell and bake for about 30 minutes or until firm and the center is set. Transfer to a wire rack and cool completely. Unmold and transfer to a plate. Serve with a dollop of whipped cream, a drizzle of molasses, and a sprinkling of pomegranate seeds.

CHOCOLATE TART
WITH PINE NUT CRUST

OCCASIONS
& THEME
PARTIES

GAME DAY FIESTA

Game on! Banish the sticky wings and heavy French onion dip in favor of a festive spread that will thrill sports fanatics and occasional fans alike. The menu takes simple Mexican favorites to unexpected heights, blending familiar flavors in a whole new way. Though most guests will focus their attention on the playing field, those who don't know a tackle from a tight end will still have plenty of fun at the fully loaded buffet table, helping themselves to savory snacks or enjoying an entire meal. Let's rewrite the party playbook.

FOOTBALL BROWNIES
(PAGE 128)

PLEASE JOIN

Joni & Eric

FOR MARGARITAS AND TACOS
AS THEY WATCH

The Big Game

SUNDAY, FEBRUARY 4TH
AT 6PM
505 10TH STREET #3F
DENVER

PLEASE REPLY

THE MENU

SIGNATURE DRINK: PASSION FRUIT
MARGARITA

APPETIZER: GUACAMOLE WITH
PISTACHIOS

SIDE DISHES: CHIPOTLE-ROASTED BABY
CARROTS WITH WATERCRESS, YOGURT,
& SESAME; GREEN HERB RICE WITH PEAS

MAIN DISH: COCHINITA PIBIL TACOS
WITH PICKLED RED ONIONS

DESSERT: FOOTBALL BROWNIES

THE SCENE

INVITATION: Choose an invitation banded with black-and-white stripes like a referee's jersey. Or, as an alternate, amplify the graphic nature of the classic football jersey with an invitation showing bold stripes in the two opposing teams' colors.

DÉCOR: Take the styling of this super-macho event in a chic new direction with a palette of deepest blues, graphite gray, and emerald green. A Belgian linen runner in midnight blue works well, as do mismatched linen napkins and tableware in blues, grays, and greens. You don't need a centerpiece here, per se, but anchoring the table with a few unexpected floral arrangements—succulents paired with deep red and dark pink ranunculus and anemones—adds a lush touch. If you want to play up the fiesta theme, order a string of cut paper party flags in dark navy to hang over the table. Scatter the table with little bowls of hot sauce and spicy pickled onions and peppers, especially condiments in the opposing teams' colors. You might also bring to the table artisanal chocolates in classically Mexican spicy-sweet flavors, or a fleet of mini hot sauce bottles (produced by every major maker). These also make great take-home gifts.

MENU: This taco recipe, made with spice-rubbed pork shoulder cooked low and slow, is simply perfect. (For vegetarians, set out spice-rubbed potatoes and squash cooked in the same way.) Be sure to provide plenty of toppings and condiments—sprigs of cilantro, wedges of lime, hot sauces, and spicy pickles—so everyone can craft their tacos to suit their tastes.

THE ACTIVITY

Invite guests to join in the competition by predicting the evening's winner. Set up a blackboard divided vertically into two columns, one for each team. Using black paper, cut out small jersey-shaped cards printing each person's initials on the front with a white marker. With a bit of double-sided tape, each guest adds his or her card to one side or to the other.

THE COUNTDOWN

3 WEEKS: Send out invitations.

2 WEEKS: Source specialty condiments, smoked sea salt for the cocktails, and chocolates. Buy cut paper flags to hang, if desired.

1 WEEK: Choose table linens, tableware, utensils and serving ware, and stark black and white vessels for flower arrangements.

4 DAYS: Pickle the onions. Stock the bar. Shop for tortilla chips, corn tortillas for the tacos, and all nonperishable items.

2 DAYS: Buy all the fresh ingredients. Purchase the fresh flowers and succulents.

DAY BEFORE: Make the achiote paste for the tacos. Bake the brownies. Arrange the flowers.

MORNING OF: Bake the pork. Rim the margarita glasses with salt. Sauté the pistachios for the guacamole. Broil and blend the chiles for the rice dish. Rearrange the furniture, if need be, creating ideal viewing and seating areas for all your guests.

3 HOURS: Lay the table. Set up glassware for the bar.

2 HOURS: Boil the rice, and roast the carrots.

1 HOUR: Lay the table, putting out the condiments.

45 MINUTES: Make the guac, and set out the chips. Shred the pork.

20 MINUTES: Plate the carrots on the yogurt. Ice the brownies.

10 MINUTES: Lay out all the taco fixings and sides. Bring ice to the bar; keep pitchers of the margarita mix and beer in an ice bath.

5 MINUTES: Turn on the game!

THE SHORTCUT

SUBSTITUTE A STORE-BOUGHT ACHIOTE PASTE in the taco recipe, or buy your pickled onions, instead of making them from scratch. You can also use a boxed mix for the brownies.

DON'T SKIMP ON THE SNACKS. Even though you're serving a whole meal, it's nice to provide a variety of snacks on the table— chili-spiced nuts, a small bowl of chocolates, maybe some sliced mango, and a few different salsas to pair with chips. In the same way, stock the bar with a range of Mexican beers.

REMEMBER TO HANDLE THE AVOCADOS CAREFULLY to avoid overmashing when making the guacamole. Use a flat-bottomed bowl, or casserole, so that you can see what you're doing. This haute dip calls for a decent chip—splurge a little on the best.

THE POUR

This luxe margarita uses fresh juice to create a dreamy, tropical flavor. But if passion fruit isn't your thing, substitute any high-acid fruit—such as Meyer lemon or blood orange.

PASSION FRUIT MARGARITA

SERVES 1
HANDS-ON 10 minutes
TOTAL 10 minutes

¼	ounce dark agave nectar
¼	ounce water
1½	ounces tequila blanco
1	ounce passion fruit juice
½	ounce fresh lemon juice
½	ounce fresh lime juice
1	lime wedge

Smoked sea salt, for garnish

1. Stir together the agave nectar and water in a cocktail shaker. Add the tequila and juices. Fill the shaker with ice and shake until well chilled, about 15 seconds.
2. Moisten half or all of the rim of a rocks glass with the lime wedge and dip in the smoked sea salt.
3. Strain the cocktail into the rocks glass, fill with ice, and garnish with the lime wedge.

GREEN HERB RICE WITH PEAS,
CHIPOTLE-ROASTED BABY
CARROTS WITH WATERCRESS,
YOGURT & SESAME (PAGE 127)

GUACAMOLE
WITH PISTACHIOS

THE RECIPES

GUACAMOLE WITH PISTACHIOS

SERVES 6
HANDS-ON 20 minutes
TOTAL 20 minutes

2   tablespoons extra-virgin olive oil
¹/₂ cup unsalted pistachios, coarsely
     chopped
Kosher salt
3   Hass avocados, halved and pitted
¹/₄ cup minced white onion, rinsed
     and blotted dry
2   jalapeños, seeded and minced
2   tablespoons fresh lime juice
¹/₂ cup chopped cilantro, plus leaves
     for garnish
Tortilla chips, for serving

I. In a medium skillet, heat the oil until shimmering. Add the pistachios and cook, stirring until lightly toasted, about 3 minutes. Using a slotted spoon, transfer the pistachios to paper towels to drain; reserve the oil in the skillet. Season the pistachios with the salt.
2. Scoop the avocados into a medium bowl, and coarsely mash with a masher or whisk.
3. Stir in the onion, jalapeños, lime juice, chopped cilantro, and all but 2 tablespoons of the pistachios; season with the salt.
4. Scrape the guacamole into a serving bowl; drizzle some reserved oil on top. Garnish with the cilantro leaves and the remaining pistachios. Serve with the tortilla chips.

GREEN HERB RICE WITH PEAS

SERVES 6 to 8
HANDS-ON 30 minutes
TOTAL I hour, 20 minutes

2   poblano chiles
I   small white onion, coarsely chopped
3   garlic cloves, sliced
I   cup chicken stock or water
I   cup packed parsley leaves
2   teaspoons kosher salt
I½ tablespoons extra-virgin olive oil
I½ cups medium-grain uncooked white rice
I   10-ounce bag frozen peas, thawed (or 2 cups fresh)

I. Preheat the broiler. Set a rack 4 inches from the heat.
2. Broil the chiles on a foil-lined baking sheet, turning occasionally, until blackened all over, about 8 minutes. Transfer the chiles to a bowl, cover with plastic wrap, and let steam for 20 minutes.
3. Peel and seed the chiles; transfer to a blender.
4. In a small saucepan, cover the onion and garlic with water; bring to a boil. Drain and transfer to the blender. Add the stock, parsley, and salt; process until smooth.
5. Heat the olive oil in a medium saucepan over medium-high. Add the rice; cook, stirring, until lightly toasted, 5 minutes. Stir in the puree and peas; bring to a simmer. Reduce the heat to low, cover, and cook for 20 minutes.
6. Remove the pan from the heat; let stand for 10 minutes. Fluff with a fork before serving.

CHIPOTLE-ROASTED BABY CARROTS WITH WATERCRESS, YOGURT & SESAME

SERVES 6
HANDS-ON 20 minutes
TOTAL I hour

30 thin baby carrots (2 to 3 bunches), scrubbed, tops trimmed
2   chipotle peppers (canned in adobo sauce), minced, plus I teaspoon sauce
I   tablespoon unsulfured molasses
2½ tablespoons extra-virgin olive oil
Table salt and black pepper
3   tablespoons sesame seeds
Plain Greek yogurt, for serving
4   ounces watercress, stems discarded

I. Preheat the oven to 350°F.
2. On a rimmed baking sheet, toss the carrots with the minced chipotles, molasses, and 2 tablespoons of the olive oil; season with the salt and pepper. Roast the carrots for 30 to 35 minutes until tender, crisp, and browned. Transfer the carrots to a plate; let cool.
3. Meanwhile, in a skillet, toast the sesame seeds over medium, tossing until golden, 3 to 5 minutes. Stir in the remaining ½ tablespoon olive oil and season with the salt; let cool.
4. Toss the carrots with the 1 teaspoon of the adobo sauce.
5. Spread a thick layer of the yogurt on a plate; top with the carrots. Scatter the watercress over the carrots. Garnish with the sesame seeds and serve with the yogurt.

COCHINITA PIBIL TACOS WITH PICKLED RED ONIONS

SERVES 6 to 8
HANDS-ON I hour, 5 minutes
TOTAL 4 hours, 35 minutes

¼   cup plus 2 tablespoons achiote seeds
2   tablespoons dried oregano, preferably Mexican
I½ tablespoons whole allspice berries
I½ tablespoons whole black peppercorns
I   3-inch cinnamon stick
30 garlic cloves (2 heads), unpeeled
I   cup apple cider vinegar
2   banana leaves (or parchment paper)
2   pounds boneless pork shoulder
Kosher salt
16 corn tortillas
Pickled Red Onions (page 128)
Salsa habañero, store-bought
I   lime, cut into wedges

I. Heat a medium-sized cast-iron skillet over medium for 5 minutes. Add the first 5 ingredients to the skillet and lightly toast, stirring, until fragrant, about 2 minutes. Transfer the spices to a small bowl, and let cool completely.
2. Working in batches using a spice grinder (or use a mortar and pestle), grind the spices to a fine powder.
3. Return the skillet to medium. Add the garlic cloves and cook, turning occasionally, until blackened in spots, 6 minutes. Remove the skillet from the heat; let the garlic cool.
4. Peel the garlic cloves; add to a blender with ground spices and vinegar. Process to a smooth paste.
5. Preheat the oven to 300°F.
6. Line a 6-quart Dutch oven with the banana leaves in a cross pattern,

letting the leaves fall over the sides of the pot (or use parchment paper). Place the pork shoulder in the pot, and season liberally with the salt. Rub 1 cup of the achiote paste all over the pork (reserve the extra paste for another use). Fold the leaves over to enclose the pork; cover the casserole.

7. Bake the pork for 3 hours until tender and a knife tip inserted in the center of the pork comes out with no resistance. Let the pork rest, covered, for 30 minutes.

8. Meanwhile, heat the cast-iron skillet over medium for 5 minutes. Place 1 tortilla in the skillet; cook, turning once, until lightly toasted and pliable, about 2 minutes. Transfer to a towel to keep warm; repeat with the remaining tortillas.

9. Transfer the pork to a cutting board and unwrap. Shred the meat with 2 forks or coarsely chop. Serve the pork in a bowl with the tortillas, pickled onions, hot sauce, and lime.

PICKLED RED ONIONS

MAKES 1½ cups
HANDS-ON 10 minutes
TOTAL 2 hours, 10 minutes

1	teaspoon coriander seeds
¼	teaspoon cumin seeds
¼	teaspoon whole black peppercorns
½	bay leaf
¾	cup apple cider vinegar
2	teaspoons sugar
2	teaspoons kosher salt
1	medium-sized red onion, thinly sliced

1. Heat a small skillet over medium for 5 minutes. Add the coriander, cumin, peppercorns, and bay leaf. Cook, stirring, until fragrant and lightly toasted, about 1 minute.

2. Add the vinegar, sugar, and salt; simmer, stirring to dissolve the sugar and salt.

3. Pour the mixture into a small heatproof bowl; stir in the onion. Cover with plastic wrap; let stand for 2 hours. The pickled onions will keep in the refrigerator for up to 1 week.

FOOTBALL BROWNIES

SERVES 10
HANDS-ON 30 minutes
TOTAL 3 hours, 40 minutes (includes cooling)

BROWNIES

12	ounces semisweet chocolate baking bar, chopped
¾	cup unsalted butter
2	ounces unsweetened chocolate baking bar, chopped
3	cups granulated sugar
4	large eggs
2	teaspoons vanilla extract
⅔	cup all-purpose flour
¼	cup unsweetened cocoa
½	teaspoon kosher salt

ICING

1	cup powdered sugar
½	teaspoon vanilla extract
1 to 2 tablespoons whole milk	

1. MAKE THE BROWNIES: Preheat the oven to 350°F. Line the bottom of a 13- x 9-inch baking pan with parchment paper, and lightly coat with cooking spray. Place the semisweet chocolate, butter, and unsweetened chocolate in the top of a double boiler. Bring the water in the bottom pan to a light boil over medium. Cook the chocolate mixture, stirring often, until melted and smooth, about 10 minutes. Cool slightly, about 10 minutes.

2. Whisk together the sugar, eggs, and vanilla in a large bowl. Add the chocolate mixture to the sugar mixture, stirring until smooth. Sift together the flour, cocoa, and salt. Stir the flour mixture into the chocolate mixture until fully incorporated. Spread the batter in the prepared pan.

3. Bake at 350°F until a wooden pick inserted in the center comes out with a few moist crumbs, 32 to 35 minutes. Cool completely in the pan on a wire rack, about 2 hours. Turn the brownies out onto a baking sheet; cut 10 (4-inch) football shapes, reserving the scraps for another use.

4. MAKE THE ICING: Whisk together the powdered sugar, vanilla, and 1 tablespoon of the milk in a medium bowl until smooth. Whisk in the remaining milk, 1 teaspoon at a time, to the desired consistency. Spoon the icing into a piping bag or a ziplock plastic bag with 1 corner snipped. Pipe the football stripes onto the brownies. Let the icing set before serving, about 20 minutes.

COCHINITA PIBIL
TACOS WITH PICKLED
RED ONIONS (PAGE 127)

TWO-CHEESE FRITTATA
WITH ARUGULA (PAGE 137)

BEST FRIENDS' BRUNCH

Rise and shine! Turn brunch into a special occasion with a pack of your beloved best friends. The supremely satisfying frittata is dotted with little pockets of creamy goat cheese and comes paired with a crisp and bright arugula salad. Roasted potatoes are done with a peppery pecorino-cheese blend, and a well-stocked DIY granola bar has something for everyone. And it's all just as inviting and delicious as it looks. The preparation is all basically stress-free, so you can spend the morning basking in the glowing company.

COME TO MY PLACE FOR A

BEST FRIENDS' BRUNCH

SUNDAY, MARCH 25TH AT 10:30 AM | JAMIE'S LOFT

THE MENU

SIGNATURE DRINK: POET'S SONG

MAIN DISH: TWO-CHEESE FRITTATA WITH ARUGULA

SALAD: ARUGULA SALAD WITH LEMONY DRESSING

SIDE DISH: CACIO E PEPE ROASTED POTATOES

THE SCENE

DÉCOR: The palette here is fresh and bright, with a lot of indigo, fuchsia, and spring-y green. Look for dyed table linens with an organic, artisanal feel, like a dotted runner, but then highlight the floral arrangements by choosing contrasting cloth napkins in deep pink. Lining up several trays along the center of the table helps define the space. Choose graphic, indigo patterned ones in laminated bamboo or melamine, if you can find them, but any trays in the saturated color palette will work just fine. Using wooden flatware and serving utensils will lend the table warmth and earthiness.

FLOWERS: These bright beauties—a mix of electric pink carnations, peonies, ranunculus, and pale green viburnum—look morning fresh tucked into glass bottles and arranged down the table's center. Add sprigs of small berries into the mix—elderberries are sweet— using miniature bottles as little bud vases to nestle in and around the granola bar.

MENU: Let each guest make a DIY bowl of granola. Start by setting out a big bowl of gourmet cereal and another of yogurt, along with a stack of smaller bowls (Japanese tea bowls work well). But then elevate the offerings with goji berries, shredded coconut, dried cherries, dried figs, and so on. If you feel inspired, set out a selection of different kinds of honey.

THE TAKE-HOME

A small jar of honey—raw, unfiltered, and bought at your local greenmarket or online from a purveyor such as TrūBee Honey (see The Resources, starting on page 180)—does double duty here, anchoring each place card and serving as a sweet take-home gift. In keeping with the laid-back indigo palette, cut rectangular tags from an old pair of jeans, printing each guest's name with a white paint marker and affixing each label to the jars with twine. If you have the time, cinch a little blossom into the tie, perfectly pulling together the whole look.

THE COUNTDOWN

3 WEEKS: Send out invitations. Order toast-shaped cork coasters. Shop for table linens, serving vessels, and yogurt bowls.

I WEEK: Buy granola, nuts, and dried fruit fixings, and sparkling wine and liquors for the cocktails. Purchase jars of honey. Find bottles for the flowers.

5 DAYS: Create denim place cards and attach them to the honey jars.

2 DAYS: Shop for fresh ingredients and flowers.

DAY BEFORE: Lay out the granola bar fixings, except the dairy items. Arrange the flowers.

NIGHT BEFORE: Toast sunflower seeds for the salad. Grate cheeses for the frittata, the potatoes, and for the salad dressing. If making a

batch of cocktails, mix the base but don't add the sparkling wine. Chill it instead. Set the table with a honey jar at each place setting.

MORNING OF: Bake the frittata. Make the salad dressing. Cut up the cherry tomatoes.

2 HOURS: Chop the potatoes.

90 MINUTES: Roast the potatoes. Set up a cocktail-making station.

30 MINUTES: Start the coffee.

15 MINUTES: Garnish the potatoes with the parsley. Toss the salad.

10 MINUTES: Set out the yogurt and milk for the coffee.

5 MINUTES: Start the music. Bring the frittata, potatoes, and salad to the table.

THE SHORTCUT

INSTEAD OF BLENDING EACH COCKTAIL INDIVIDUALLY, make the base the day before and set it out chilled in a pitcher, adding sparkling wine at the bar.

PICK UP A RANGE OF SWEET AND SAVORY BAKED ITEMS at your favorite local pastry shop, rounding out the selection if you're expecting a crowd. (Remember to set out a little jam and butter too.)

IF THIS IS AN ALL-FEMALE GATHERING, make a playlist of female vocalists.

YOU'D NEVER SERVE COLD SCRAMBLED EGGS, but frittata dished up at room temperature is every bit as delicious as when it's piping hot. One way to guarantee success is by cooking it in clarified butter, which burns at a higher temperature and will keep the dish from tasting smoky or overdone.

A BIG STACK OF MAGAZINES OR ROLLED NEWSPAPERS nestled into a big wooden serving bowl gives each friend a nice treat on the way out.

THE POUR

This grown-up, daytime cocktail is flavored with a wintry mix of apple cider, maple syrup, and cinnamon. Serve on a clever faux-toast coaster made from a slice of cork and found at momastore.org.

POET'S SONG

SERVES I
HANDS-ON 3 minutes
TOTAL 3 minutes

1½   ounces spiced apple cider, well chilled
¾   ounce Becherovka liqueur (a cinnamon-scented brew) or Hiram Walker Cinnamon Schnapps
⅛   ounce maple syrup
Sparkling wine
Apple slices (optional)

Pour the cider, liqueur, and syrup into a goblet and stir. Top with the sparkling wine. Garnish with the apple slices, if desired.

ARUGULA SALAD
WITH LEMONY DRESSING
(PAGE 137); POET'S SONG

CACIO E PEPE
ROASTED POTATOES

THE RECIPES

TWO-CHEESE FRITTATA WITH ARUGULA

SERVES 4 to 6
HANDS-ON 17 minutes
TOTAL 45 minutes

SALAD

1/3 cup sunflower seeds, for toasting
2 cups baby arugula
Juice of 1/2 small lemon
2 tablespoons extra-virgin olive oil
Sea salt, to taste
Freshly ground black pepper

FRITTATA

12 large eggs, beaten
2 tablespoons unsalted butter or olive oil
1 cup packed arugula
3 ounces Gruyère or Comté cheese, coarsely grated
3 ounces goat cheese, crumbled

1. MAKE THE SALAD: Position the rack in the center of the oven; preheat to 350°F. Toast the sunflower seeds on a baking sheet for about 10 minutes, being careful not to burn them.
2. MAKE THE FRITTATA: In a large bowl, whisk the eggs.
3. In a 10-inch nonstick ovenproof skillet, heat 1 tablespoon of the butter over medium. Add the arugula; cook for 1 minute.
4. Add the remaining 1 tablespoon butter and eggs; immediately reduce the heat to medium-low.
5. Cook for 8 to 10 minutes until the bottom sets and the top is partially set.
6. Sprinkle on the cheeses; let the edges set (1 to 2 minutes). It should look shiny and uncooked on top, with the cheeses still unmelted.

7. Bake in the oven for 8 minutes, until the cheese melts and the frittata puffs slightly.
8. Meanwhile, toss the arugula, lemon juice, oil, salt, and pepper.
9. Cut the frittata into wedges, top with the salad, and sprinkle with the toasted sunflower seeds before serving.

ARUGULA SALAD WITH LEMONY DRESSING

SERVES 6
HANDS-ON 10 minutes
TOTAL 10 minutes

1/3 cup extra-virgin olive oil
1 tablespoon lemon zest, plus 3 tablespoons fresh juice (from about 2 lemons)
1 teaspoon kosher salt
1 teaspoon Dijon mustard
1 teaspoon honey
1/4 teaspoon black pepper
2 ounces fresh Parmesan cheese, grated
2 teaspoons fresh thyme leaves
1 (5-ounce) package baby arugula
1 cup halved cherry tomatoes

1. Process the oil, lemon zest, lemon juice, salt, mustard, honey, pepper, and 1/4 cup of the Parmesan in a food processor until smooth, about 10 seconds. Stir in the thyme leaves.
2. Combine the arugula and tomatoes in large bowl. Toss with 3 tablespoons of the dressing to coat. Divide the arugula mixture among 6 salad plates; sprinkle with the remaining 1/4 cup Parmesan, and serve immediately with the remaining dressing.

CACIO E PEPE ROASTED POTATOES

SERVES 4
HANDS-ON 12 minutes
TOTAL 1 hour, 7 minutes

2 pounds medium-sized red potatoes (about 9)
1 teaspoon kosher salt
6 tablespoons extra-virgin olive oil
1 tablespoon white wine vinegar
1 1/2 teaspoons black pepper
1/2 teaspoon Dijon mustard
1 ounce pecorino Romano cheese, grated, plus more for garnish
1/4 ounce Parmigiano-Reggiano cheese, grated, plus more for garnish
Chopped fresh parsley (optional)

1. Preheat the oven to 425°F. Cut the potatoes in half lengthwise; cut each half lengthwise into 3 wedges (about 1 inch thick). Toss the potato wedges with the salt and 2 tablespoons of the oil on a large rimmed baking sheet.
2. Bake at 425°F until the potatoes are deep golden brown, 35 to 40 minutes, stirring twice with a metal spatula during baking to brown on all sides. Remove from oven and cool 20 minutes.
3. Whisk together the vinegar, pepper, mustard, and remaining 1/4 cup oil in a medium bowl until well blended; whisk in the cheeses. Add the potatoes, and toss to coat. Sprinkle with the parsley and cheeses, if desired, and serve immediately.

AWARDS NIGHT BASH

Nothing quite compares to the glamour of old Hollywood—why not capture that refined ambiance with black-and-white décor and a menu of elevated treats? A Spicy Pear-Tini, of course, pays homage to the ritzy cocktail of yore with a stylish twist. While the stars take the stage, you'll dazzle at home. This fete is all fun, no-stress with everything falling into place well before the red carpet arrivals start.

CARAMELIZED ONION
& GOAT CHEESE TARTS
(PAGE 144)

AND THE AWARD GOES TO...

SAGE & SAM DALLOWAY

FOR THROWING A

CRITICALLY ACCLAIMED

AWARDS NIGHT
PARTY

SUNDAY, MARCH 4TH

OUR PLACE | 7PM

SMALL BITES & COCKTAILS

ATTIRE: GLITZ & GLAM | RSVP

THE MENU

SIGNATURE DRINK: SPICY PEAR-TINI

HORS D'OEUVRES: CARAMELIZED
ONION & GOAT CHEESE TARTS; CREAMY
CARROT SOUP SHOOTERS

DESSERT: BLACK & WHITE COOKIES

THE SCENE

INVITATION: An invitation showcasing the iconic ceremonial spotlight lets guests know it will be an evening of refined fun. Choose a classic design, boasting black and white to match the party's color palette.

DÉCOR: Black and white—on a neutral gray tablecloth—and nothing more. Natural materials—like ceramic, slate, and soapstone—all in alabaster white and matte black—lend the array sensuous drama, as do a variety of serving dishes in marble. To vary the display, use cake stands for height, or overturn a bowl to use as a riser. Then, to keep things from getting too serious, bring in a few swirly patterned balloons. Olive branches breathe an earthy freshness into the display (though palm fronds evoke the California vibe well too) while sweet white anemones tucked into small vases promote the bicolored theme beautifully. You might even play up the filmic angle by uncoiling rolls of 35mm camera film and arranging the dark tendrils along the table's center.

MENU: There's an unapologetic luxury in this selection—rich delicacies presented without a lot of tricky sleight of hand. Flaky mini-tarts, iced cookies, and carrot soup shooters satisfy, while additional store-bought treats such as dark chocolate, luscious grapes and figs, and sumptuous cheeses never looked more irresistible than when played off the stark two-toned palette. It all works especially well with sparkling wine.

THE ACTIVITY

Everyone wins when playing the Oscar lottery—especially if the prize is a bottle of Champagne. Find downloadable ballots online to use as a template, but do take the time to personalize yours, printing them on nice heavy stock or foil-flecked stationery. Team up film aficionados with less confident players to ensure fun for all. If kids are coming, provide an activity for them as well to keep them entertained. Set out cording, scissors, and a bowl of alphabet beads, and invite them to make bracelets, necklaces, and key chains of their own design.

THE COUNTDOWN

3 WEEKS: Send out invitations.

2 WEEKS: Order stationery supplies for the ballots, including pencils and, if desired, clipboards for supporting the ballots. Order 35mm film for the table display. Stock up on cocktail supplies and sparkling wines. Determine which serving vessels will suit each dish. Buy tablewares, linens, glassware, and balloons.

1 WEEK: Print out the Oscar ballots for the activity. Select an outfit for the evening, something black and white or something that shimmers with Hollywood glam.

2 DAYS: Bake the cookies, storing them in an airtight container.

DAY BEFORE: Whip up the icing and ice the cookies. Make the soup, and refrigerate. Rim the cocktail glasses with cinnamon sugar. Begin setting up the buffet. Arrange the viewing area, making sure there are cozy places to sit.

5 HOURS: Plate the cookies. Set up the martini bar. Thaw the puff pastry dough. Bring the goat cheese to room temperature.

1 HOUR: Lay out any extra nibbles like chocolate, cheese, and fruit. Put the sparkling wine on ice.

45 MINUTES: Bake the caramelized onion tarts.

30 MINUTES: Bring the tarts to the table. Reheat the soup. Slice the pears for the cocktail garnish.

5 MINUTES: Turn on the show!

THE SHORTCUT

YOU COULD GO STORE-BOUGHT, shopping for everything offered in this spread—tarts, soup, and cookies. Still it's nice to make one dish from scratch, if possible.

FREEZE THE COOKIE DOUGH in advance, cutting off rounds to bake when you're ready. Roll the dough into a cylindrical shape and wrap tightly with wax paper. Store in a freezer bag up to 3 months.

BLEND THE COCKTAIL BASE in advance, serving it from a tall and slim cylindrical pitcher or beaker.

DECK THE TABLE with a slew of black-and-white treats, from swirly lollipops and candy swizzle sticks to black-and-white macarons (a more special choice than Oreos).

NO TIME FOR HELIUM BALLOONS? You can fake the look by using a super-skinny dowel rod to hold the balloon and disguising it slightly by winding a thin ribbon or butcher's twine around the stick.

THE POUR

The swanky martini is softened and rounded out with a spicy-fruity approach, incorporating the unexpected scent of pear.

SPICY PEAR-TINI

SERVES 1
HANDS-ON 3 minutes
TOTAL 3 minutes

1 ounce pear vodka or pear brandy
1 ounce spiced rum
1 ounce pear nectar, apple juice, or orange juice
Cinnamon sugar
Sliced pear (optional)

Combine the pear vodka or pear brandy, spiced rum, and pear nectar, apple juice, or orange juice in an ice-filled shaker. Shake vigorously, and strain into a cocktail glass rimmed with cinnamon sugar. Garnish with a sliced pear, if desired.

CREAMY CARROT
SOUP SHOOTERS
(PAGE 144)

THE RECIPES

CARAMELIZED ONION & GOAT CHEESE TARTS

SERVES 8
HANDS-ON 36 minutes
TOTAL 50 minutes

1   tablespoon unsalted butter
1   large onion, thinly sliced
¼   cup water
½   teaspoon chopped fresh thyme leaves, plus more for garnish
1   puff pastry sheet, thawed (from a 17.3-ounce package frozen puff pastry sheets)
1   (4-ounce) log fresh mild goat cheese, at room temperature

1. Center a rack in the oven and preheat to 450°F.
2. In a heavy skillet, melt the butter over medium-high. Sauté the onion, stirring occasionally, until golden, about 15 minutes.
3. Add the water and deglaze the skillet, loosening any brown bits and cooking until the water evaporates. Stir in the thyme and cook until the onion is a deeper brown, about 10 minutes.
4. While the onion is cooking, cut off ⅓ of the pastry sheet, cutting lengthwise along the perforated line. Halve the piece again lengthwise to create 2 (10- x 3-inch) strips. Cut each strip into 8 triangles.
5. Place the triangles on a parchment paper-lined baking sheet, prick the pastry all over with a fork; bake until golden, about 10 minutes.
6. Spread the goat cheese onto the triangles; top with the onions.
7. Garnish with the fresh thyme leaves and serve immediately.

CARAMELIZED ONION & GOAT CHEESE TARTS

CREAMY CARROT SOUP SHOOTERS

SERVES 12
HANDS-ON 15 minutes
TOTAL 25 minutes

2   tablespoons olive oil
3   cups sliced peeled carrots (about 1 pound)
½   cup sliced Vidalia or other sweet onion (from 1 small onion)
2   fresh thyme sprigs
3   cups unsalted chicken stock
½   teaspoon kosher salt
½   teaspoon black pepper
⅓   cup heavy cream
½   cup finely chopped salted, roasted pistachios

1. Heat the oil in a medium saucepan over medium-high. Add the carrots, onion slices, and thyme sprigs, and cover. Reduce the heat to medium, and cook, stirring occasionally, until the vegetables just begin to soften, about 8 minutes.
2. Stir in the stock, salt, and pepper. Cover and cook until the carrots and onions are very soft, about 10 minutes. Remove and discard the thyme sprigs.
3. Transfer the mixture to a blender, and add the cream. Remove the center piece of the blender lid (to allow the steam to escape); secure the lid on the blender, and place a clean towel over the opening in the lid. Process until smooth.
4. Divide the soup among the shot glasses, and sprinkle with the pistachios before serving.

BLACK & WHITE COOKIES

SERVES 24
HANDS-ON 30 minutes
TOTAL 1 hour, 30 minutes

COOKIES

4	cups unbleached cake flour
1/2	teaspoon baking powder
1/2	teaspoon table salt
1 3/4	cups granulated sugar
1	cup unsalted butter, softened
2	large eggs, at room temperature
1/2	teaspoon vanilla extract
1/4	teaspoon lemon extract
1	cup whole milk

ICING

3	cups powdered sugar
3	tablespoons meringue powder
4 to 6	tablespoons water
2	tablespoons special dark chocolate cocoa (such as Hershey's Special Dark Cocoa)

1. MAKE THE COOKIES: Position the oven racks in the upper and lower thirds of the oven, and preheat the oven to 375°F. Line 2 baking sheets with parchment paper.
2. Combine the flour, baking powder, and salt in a medium bowl. Combine the sugar and butter in the bowl of a stand mixer fitted with the paddle attachment, and beat on medium speed until light and fluffy, about 2 minutes. Add the eggs, vanilla, and lemon extract; beat on low speed until combined, about 30 seconds, stopping to scrape the sides of the bowl if necessary. Add the flour mixture to the sugar mixture alternately with the milk, beginning and ending with the flour mixture. Beat on low speed until fully combined after each addition, stopping to scrape the sides and bottom of the bowl as needed.

3. Scoop ¼-cupfuls of batter onto the prepared baking sheets. Bake in the preheated oven until the cookies are firm and the edges are lightly browned, 18 to 20 minutes, switching the pans top rack to bottom rack after 10 minutes. Cool the cookies on the baking sheets about 2 minutes; transfer the cookies to a wire rack to cool completely, about 20 minutes.
4. MAKE THE ICING: Combine 2 cups of the powdered sugar and 2 tablespoons of the meringue powder in a medium bowl. Add 2 tablespoons of the water, stirring until the mixture reaches spreading consistency. (Stir in more water, 1 teaspoon at a time, if necessary, to reach the desired consistency.) Combine the cocoa, remaining 1 cup powdered sugar, and remaining 1 tablespoon meringue powder in a separate bowl. Add 2 tablespoons of the water, stirring until the mixture reaches spreading consistency. (Stir in more water, 1 teaspoon at a time, if necessary, to reach the desired consistency.) Using a small offset spatula, spread the white icing over the bottom (flat part) of each cookie. Let stand until the white icing is set, about 10 minutes. Spread the chocolate icing over half of the white icing. Let stand until set, about 20 more minutes.

BLACK & WHITE COOKIES

WOODLAND BABY SHOWER

Cast a spell, throwing a baby shower that's as lively and lush as a fairy-tale fantasy. A wild and wooded décor brings an enchanted tablescape to life. A vivid tableau vivant of delicate leafy foliage and sweet woodland creatures is designed to stir the imagination. Caramel apples shine on a rustic wooden platter. A selection of savory mini-quiches and a galette tempts one and all, while Mulled Cranberry Wine Punch scents the air with spicy sweetness. Most magical of all is a breathtaking chocolate roulade flavored with coffee and overgrown with perky meringue mushrooms. What a romantic way to welcome a little sprite!

MINI BACON QUICHES
(PAGE 152)

Join us for a baby shower
in honor of

Josephine
Taylor

Sunday, March 31st at 2pm
at the home of Shaun Dorough
#2 Pine View Road

Please reply by March 24th

THE MENU

SIGNATURE DRINK: MULLED
CRANBERRY WINE PUNCH

HORS D'OEUVRES: MINI BACON
QUICHES; MUSHROOM & BUTTERNUT
SQUASH GALETTE

DESSERT: CHOCOLATE-COFFEE
ROULADE

THE SCENE

DÉCOR: Conjuring up this dreamy deep-woods wonderland is not as complicated as it might seem, once you've assembled the basics. Start with a live moss tablerunner or stagger small pots of moss along the tablescape. Incorporate greenery such as clumps of maidenhair ferns and bramble branches in earth-toned or wooden vessels. For pops of color to complement the forested effect, you might add mini-orchids. Fresh-cut wood rounds in different widths vary the display heights. To go the extra mile, purchase bark-covered pillar candles and wax pinecone-shaped candles. Scatter acorn chocolates along the length of the table as if they'd simply dropped there. Or, skip the candles and chocolates, and source pinecones, small logs, and acorns from the woods. And the final touch—for cuteness sake!—is to invite in a little forest friend or two.

CENTERPIECE: Assemble a mini still life under a glass cloche with folksy faux wooden mushrooms, a ruby-red pomegranate, and a woodland creature or two.

MENU: Beguile guests with creamy mini-quiches, a savory galette, and shining caramel apples. Serving mulled wine in clear glass mugs shows off the beautiful, dark color of the brew, while cinnamon sticks make perfect stirrers. If you like, it's fun to tuck in little packets of shortbread bunnies, deer, and leaf-shaped cookies along the table. To bring a woodsy look to store-bought cupcakes, decorate the iced tops with dark chocolate leaves.

THE ACTIVITY

Transform your guests into tree sprites with leafy fairy crowns of their own. Create the crown foundations in advance by intertwining several lengths of lightweight wire into a circle using pliers, or use the inner rings of wooden embroidery hoops (about 7 or 8 inches in diameter). Cover the wires or hoops with wound ribbon, leaving a long length on each side. At the party, inspire guests to complete their crowns with velvet leaves, satin ribbons, silk flowers, and tiny spun-cotton mushrooms. (Affixing these bits and bobs with a glue gun works well.)

THE COUNTDOWN

6 WEEKS: Send out invitations hinting at your woodsy theme.

2 WEEKS: Choose something romantic and soft to wear. Buy wood rounds, a glass cloche, serving vessels, and props. Decide on tableware and glassware.

1 WEEK: Order supplemental pastries, iced cookies, or meringue mushrooms in advance. Buy ingredients for mulled wine, plus all nonperishable grocery items. Purchase everything needed for fairy crowns, including wire, decorations, ribbon, and glue.

3 DAYS: Make fairy crown bases.

2 DAYS: Shop for fresh grocery items, moss, ferns, and orchids. Prepare frosting for the roulade.

DAY BEFORE: Make the mulled wine base, without adding the wine, and chill. Bake and assemble the roulade; chill overnight.

NIGHT BEFORE: Begin to arrange the tablescape, laying out the verdant runner and staging the biggest props. Set up the fairy crown-making area.

MORNING OF: Bake the mini-quiches and the galette.

3 HOURS: Blend and cook the mulled wine base with the wine.

30 MINUTES: Rewarm the quiches, galette, and mulled wine. Bring the roulade to the table.

10 MINUTES: Plate up the savory baked goods. Top the mini-quiches with sour cream and chopped fresh chives. Garnish the galette with fresh thyme leaves.

THE SHORTCUT

ORDER THE ROULADE from a fine pastry shop. You can still savor the fun of decorating it with old-fashioned marzipan trimmings and meringue mushrooms.

FORGO THE MOSS, layering delicate fern fronds down the center of the table instead.

IF MAKING THE CARAMEL APPLES YOURSELF, use sturdy twigs as sticks, for another rustic touch. Use a utility knife to sharpen one end to a point in order to insert it into the apple core.

MINI-ORCHIDS make a great party favor, if fairy crowns aren't your thing. Small potted phalaenopsis are a good choice, especially in deep purple and pale green. They're the easiest orchids to grow, so they'll be less intimidating to novice home gardeners. Use the plants to decorate the tabletop, but label each with a pretty gift tag-to-go.

THE POUR

Warming in every way, this spicy mulled punch brings together favorite autumnal flavors.

MULLED CRANBERRY WINE PUNCH

SERVES 12 to 14
HANDS-ON 7 minutes
TOTAL 32 minutes

1   cup fresh or frozen cranberries
1   (48-ounce) bottle cranberry juice cocktail
1/2 cup raisins
4 to 6 cinnamon sticks (about 3 inches), plus more for garnish
2   (750-milliliter) bottles fruity dry red wine such as Gamay Beaujolais, or 6 cups apple juice and 2 to 4 tablespoons lemon juice, to taste
1/4 to 1/2 cup sugar
1   teaspoon almond extract
About 3/4 cup orange liqueur such as Cointreau or triple sec (optional)

1. Sort the cranberries, discarding the bruised and decayed fruit. Rinse the berries and put in a 5- to 6-quart pan; add the cranberry juice cocktail, raisins, and cinnamon sticks. Bring to a boil over high; cover and simmer on low to blend the flavors, about 20 minutes.
2. Add the wine and 1/4 to 1/2 cup sugar, to taste. Heat until steaming, 5 to 8 minutes; do not boil.
3. Add the almond extract and orange liqueur; keep the punch warm over low and ladle into cups or stemmed glasses. Garnish with extra cinnamon sticks, if desired.

CHOCOLATE-COFFEE ROULADE
(PAGE 153); MULLED CRANBERRY
WINE PUNCH

THE RECIPES

MINI BACON QUICHES

MAKES about 2½ dozen
HANDS-ON 12 minutes
TOTAL 34 minutes

1   large red-skinned potato, peeled and diced
6   large eggs
6   bacon slices, cooked until crisp and finely chopped
2   scallions, thinly sliced (about ⅓ cup)
½   cup grated Parmesan cheese
1   teaspoon minced fresh thyme
½   teaspoon table salt
¼   teaspoon black pepper
⅓   cup sour cream
Garnishes: fresh thyme leaves, chopped fresh chives

1. Preheat the oven to 375°F. Cook the potatoes in boiling salted water to cover 8 to 10 minutes or until tender. Drain.
2. Combine the eggs and the next 6 ingredients in a medium bowl; whisk until well blended. Stir in the potato.
3. Spoon about 1 tablespoon of the egg mixture into each cup of a lightly greased miniature muffin pan. Bake 13 to 15 minutes or until lightly browned. Cool in the pans on wire racks for 5 minutes. Remove from the pans; top each quiche with about ½ teaspoon of the sour cream, and garnish, if desired. Serve the quiches warm or at room temperature.

MUSHROOM & BUTTERNUT SQUASH GALETTE

MUSHROOM & BUTTERNUT SQUASH GALETTE

SERVES 8
HANDS-ON 30 minutes
TOTAL 55 minutes

2   tablespoons olive oil
1   cup sliced Vidalia or other sweet onion (from 1 small onion)
1   (8-ounce) package sliced cremini mushrooms
2   teaspoons chopped garlic (about 2 garlic cloves)
2   teaspoons chopped fresh thyme, plus leaves for garnish
3   cups cubed peeled butternut squash (about 1 pound)
1   teaspoon kosher salt
½   teaspoon black pepper
¼   cup dry white wine (optional)
All-purpose flour, for dusting
1   (14.1-ounce) package refrigerated piecrusts
2   ounces fresh Parmesan cheese, shredded (about ½ cup)
1   large egg
1   teaspoon water

1. Preheat the oven to 400°F. Heat the oil in a large skillet over medium-high. Add the onion, mushrooms, garlic, and chopped thyme; cook, stirring occasionally, until the vegetables are browned and tender, 8 to 10 minutes. Add the squash, salt, and pepper to the skillet; reduce the heat, and cook, stirring occasionally, until the squash is tender, 6 to 8 minutes. Add the wine, if desired;

cook, stirring occasionally, until the liquid evaporates, about 1 minute. Spread the mixture on a baking sheet; let cool about 10 minutes. **2.** Line a large baking sheet with parchment paper; lightly dust with flour. Unroll the piecrusts, and stack on the prepared baking sheet. Roll into an 18-inch circle. Spread the vegetable mixture in the center of the stacked piecrusts, leaving a 3-inch border; sprinkle with the Parmesan. Fold over the edges of the dough to partially cover the filling. Whisk together the egg and water. Brush the dough with the egg mixture. Bake in the preheated oven until well browned, 25 to 30 minutes. Garnish with the thyme leaves.

CHOCOLATE-COFFEE ROULADE

SERVES 8 to 10
HANDS-ON 45 minutes
TOTAL 2 hours

CAKE
- ³/₄ cup all-purpose flour
- 2 teaspoons instant espresso granules
- 1 teaspoon baking powder
- ¹/₄ teaspoon table salt
- ¹/₃ cup plus 2 tablespoons unsweetened cocoa
- 5 large eggs, separated
- ²/₃ cup granulated sugar
- 1 tablespoon unsalted butter, melted and cooled
- 1 teaspoon vanilla extract
- 2 tablespoons powdered sugar

FILLING
- 7 tablespoons coffee liqueur
- 1 cup cold heavy cream
- ¹/₄ cup granulated sugar

FROSTING
- 1¹/₄ cups powdered sugar
- 5 tablespoons unsalted butter, softened
- 3 tablespoons unsweetened cocoa
- 2 tablespoons heavy cream
- 1¹/₂ tablespoons light corn syrup
- 1 teaspoon vanilla extract
- Meringue mushrooms (optional)

1. MAKE THE CAKE: Preheat the oven to 350°F. Coat a 15½- x 10½-inch jelly-roll pan with baking spray. Line the bottom of the pan with parchment paper or wax paper; coat the paper with baking spray. Combine the flour, instant espresso, baking powder, salt, and ⅓ cup of the cocoa in a bowl; stir with a whisk.
2. Beat the egg yolks in a large bowl with an electric mixer on medium speed until thick and pale, 2 to 3 minutes. Gradually beat in ⅓ cup of the granulated sugar. Beat in the melted butter and vanilla.
3. Using a whisk attachment, beat the egg whites with an electric mixer on medium-high speed until medium peaks form. Gradually add the remaining ⅓ cup granulated sugar, 1 tablespoon at a time. Beat on high speed until stiff peaks form. (Do not overbeat.) Stir one-fourth of the egg whites into the egg yolk mixture. Fold in the remaining egg whites. Sift the flour mixture over the top; gently fold in the flour mixture, being careful not to deflate the egg mixture. Spread the batter in the prepared jelly-roll pan. Bake in the preheated oven until the cake just begins to pull away from the edges of the pan, 8 to 10 minutes.
4. Sprinkle the powdered sugar on a clean, lint-free kitchen towel. Loosen the cake from the sides of the pan, and turn the cake out onto the prepared towel. Peel off and discard the parchment paper. Sprinkle the cake with the remaining 2 tablespoons cocoa. Starting at the short end, roll up the cake and towel together, jelly-roll fashion. Place on a wire rack, and cool completely, about 1 hour.
5. MAKE THE FILLING: Reserve ¼ cup of the liqueur for Step 7. Beat the cream, sugar, and remaining 3 tablespoons liqueur in a large bowl with an electric mixer on high speed until doubled in volume, 3 to 4 minutes. Refrigerate until ready to use.
6. MAKE THE FROSTING: Beat the powdered sugar, softened butter, and cocoa on low speed until smooth, about 2 minutes. Add the cream, corn syrup, and vanilla; beat on low speed until well combined, about 1 minute. (Frosting can be prepared up to 3 days ahead, and stored, covered, in the refrigerator. Bring to room temperature before using.)
7. To assemble the roulade, carefully unroll the cake onto the work surface; remove the towel. Brush the remaining ¼ cup liqueur over the top of the cake. Spread the Filling over the surface of the cake to within ½ inch of the edges. Reroll the cake, and place, seam side down, on the serving plate. Spread the Frosting over the top and sides of the cake roll, leaving the ends uncovered. Trim the ends, if desired. Decorate with meringue mushrooms, if desired.

SUMMER
PARTIES

TOMATO, AVOCADO
& RED ONION SALAD
(PAGE 162)

FRESH SUMMER SUPPER

At the height of the season, this sunny meal is everything you've been waiting for. It's made with a gorgeous selection of vegetables so fresh and flavorful that you don't really need to do much except let them shine. Take a simple approach at your next alfresco fete, serving guests dishes that celebrate the season's bounty—from heirloom tomatoes to sweet corn to grilled fresh fish served in a laid-back atmosphere that never distracts from the company. Just let the summertime do its thing while you kick back and relax.

FRANKIES CORN
SALAD (PAGE 162)

Summer Supper

JOIN US FOR DRINKS AND A MEAL

ON THE PATIO

SATURDAY, JUNE 16TH

AT 6:00PM

AT THE MACBETHS'

1 MAYFAIR ROAD

rsvp

THE MENU

SIGNATURE DRINKS: FRANKIES
LEMONADE; PATIO PUNCH

SALADS: FRANKIES CORN SALAD;
TOMATO, AVOCADO & RED ONION
SALAD

SIDE DISH: GRILLED VEGETABLES

MAIN DISHES: LEMONY SARDINES;
SLOW-ROASTED RIB EYE, SLICED COLD

DESSERT: OLIVE OIL CAKE WITH
BERRIES & CREAM

THE SCENE

INVITATION: Choose a leafy invitation to highlight the party's garden-fresh feel and remember to let guests know they'll be spending the evening outdoors, so they can dress accordingly.

MENU: The menu is light and super casual, just like the mini Bundt cake dessert, which makes a perfect breakfast, on the rare occasion that there are any left! A fresh tomato salad, inspired by the flavors of classic gazpacho, shows off summer's unmistakable sweet-tart deliciousness. To keep grilled corn, vegetables, and fish just as tasty, use charcoal instead of gas, and grill the corn, then the fish, then the meat, in that order, so that you avoid picking up any overwhelming flavors from the grill itself.

DÉCOR: The overall ambiance is unfussy. Nothing should divert friends' attention from the colorful allure of the ingredients or from the natural setting itself. Using only a few wildflowers arranged in minimalistic clear bottles enhances the beauty of the environment rather than competes with it. In the same way, outdoor lighting should be straightforward and pretty. Try a scattering of votive candles housed in hanging glass lanterns. And always arrange chairs near the grilling area so that guests feel that they are a part of the action.

THE ACTIVITY

While shopping at the farmers' market, search out some additional berries, cherry tomatoes, and fresh herbs, snapping up an extra bushel or two for your guests to take home. Dole out the garden-fresh goodies into small, traditional wooden pint baskets, including a small bunch of twine-tied herbs in each, and tie each basket with a blue linen ribbon. If you like, label each little basket with a brown paper gift tag that reads "bon appétit!"

THE COUNTDOWN

3 WEEKS: Send out invitations.

10 DAYS: Purchase any outdoor necessities, such as extra seating, bottles for flowers, votive candles, hanging lanterns, wooden serving planks, or an urn for the punch. Choose the simplest tableware.

5 DAYS: Buy nonperishable items, like olive oil and vinegar, and charcoal for the grill.

2 DAYS: Shop for fresh ingredients, including vegetables, fish, and meat; refrigerate. Buy fresh wildflowers. Bake the rib eye; refrigerate.

DAY BEFORE: Set up the outdoor area, including seating and lighting. Boil strawberries for the punch. Cut up the garnish for the Patio Punch (page 161). Juice the lemons for both drinks.

MORNING OF: Bake the mini-cakes. Boil simple syrup for the lemonade. Set up the grill. Arrange the flowers and bring to the table.

2 HOURS: Make the two fruit drinks and refrigerate.

I HOUR: Fire up the grill. Slice up the vegetables. Cut up the cherry tomatoes for the salad; refrigerate.

30 MINUTES: Soak the corn.

45 MINUTES: Plate the cakes and berries, but don't yet top with the crème fraîche.

10 MINUTES: Set out the fruit punches and ice. Light the candles.

AS GUESTS ARRIVE: Start grilling. Slice the rib eye; bring it to the table.

DURING THE MEAL: Dress the mini-cakes with crème fraîche and garnish with the mint.

THE SHORTCUT

AS AN ALTERNATIVE to cutting up all those vegetables on your own, put friends to work washing and chopping as they arrive. Be sure to have enough cutting boards and paring knives so that they can easily jump into the action.

TRY TURNING ITALIAN SAUSAGE into spiraled pinwheel shapes, just for fun, and grilling them for a few minutes per side to serve on a burger bun.

CHOOSE A CRISP ROSÉ to pair with these dishes, emphasizing their freshness and light flavors.

SET UP SEATING IN THE SHADE, and at a little distance from the center of the scene so that guests can escape the heat or slink away from the crowd for a quiet chat.

BAKE ONE LARGER CAKE TO SHARE, if the thought of making a fleet of mini-cakes feels daunting.

THE POUR

These icy drinks take that classic summertime combination—fresh fruit juice and a hint of fizz—in two fabulous new directions.

FRANKIES LEMONADE

SERVES 6
HANDS-ON 10 minutes
TOTAL 10 minutes

- 6   fresh lemons
- ³/₄   cup agave nectar (or simple syrup: heat equal parts water and sugar until sugar dissolves; cool)
- 6   leafy mint sprigs
- 6   cups ice cubes

Water or, preferably, sparkling water

Juice the lemons into a pitcher. Add the sweetener, mint, and ice. Stir, just so the ingredients get a chance to mingle. Top off with water and serve.

PATIO PUNCH

SERVES 6
HANDS-ON 36 minutes
TOTAL 36 minutes (includes syrup)

STRAWBERRY SYRUP

1¼	cups water
1	cup strawberries
1¼	cups sugar

Fresh lime juice

PUNCH

1½	cups light rum
½	cup Navan vanilla cognac
3	ounces amaretto
1	cup Strawberry Syrup
1¼	cups lemon juice
½	pound fresh strawberries, sliced

Lemon wheels and rosemary sprigs

1	bottle chilled Prosecco

1. MAKE THE STRAWBERRY SYRUP:
Bring the water to a boil, add the strawberries and sugar, lower to medium, and stir occasionally for 5 minutes. Strain and add a touch of the lime juice to make the flavors pop.
2. MAKE THE PUNCH: In a punch bowl, combine all the ingredients except the Prosecco. Pour into ice-filled glasses; top off with the Prosecco.

THE RECIPES

FRANKIES CORN SALAD

SERVES 6
HANDS-ON 18 minutes
TOTAL 43 minutes

4   ears of corn
1   pint cherry tomatoes, halved
2   tablespoons mint leaves, torn
½   medium-sized red onion, sliced
3   tablespoons olive oil
1   lemon, juiced
Big pinch of table salt
Crushed red pepper flakes
Castelrosso or mild provolone cheese
      (optional)

1. Preheat the grill to 450°F.
2. Soak the ears of corn in a bowl of water for 10 to 15 minutes. Peel back the husks, remove the silk, and pull the husks back over to cover the corn kernels while cooking.
3. Grill the corn for 5 minutes.
4. Remove the corn from the grill, and when they're cool enough to handle, peel off the husks. Scrape the kernels off the cobs and place in a big salad bowl.
5. Toss the tomatoes in with the corn. Add the mint and onion.
6. Dress with the olive oil, lemon juice, salt, and red pepper flakes to taste. Crumble the cheese on top.

TOMATO, AVOCADO & RED ONION SALAD

SERVES 6
HANDS-ON 13 minutes
TOTAL 13 minutes

1   pint cherry tomatoes, cut into
      wedges
1   small red onion, thinly sliced
Fine sea salt
¼   cup extra-virgin olive oil, plus
      2 tablespoons, plus more for
      drizzling
3   tablespoons red wine vinegar
3   ripe Hass avocados
Black pepper

1. In a large bowl, combine the tomatoes, onion slices, a big pinch of the salt, oil, and vinegar. Gently toss.
2. Halve, pit, and slice the avocados; divide among the plates.
3. Sprinkle each plate with a small pinch of the salt and drizzle with the olive oil. Finish with a few grinds of black pepper just before serving.

GRILLED
VEGETABLES

LEMONY SARDINES

SERVES 6
HANDS-ON 12 minutes
TOTAL 12 minutes

3/4   cup extra-virgin olive oil
1/2   cup lemon juice
Parsley leaves, finely chopped
Table salt and black pepper
18   whole sardines, with bones

1. Preheat the grill to high (450° to 550°F). Whisk together the oil, lemon juice, parsley, and salt and pepper to taste. Set aside.
2. Grill the sardines over high, skin side down, 4 to 6 minutes. Remove and brush liberally with the lemony dressing. Serve with the dressing.

GRILLED VEGETABLES

SERVES 6
HANDS-ON 1 hour, 2 minutes
TOTAL 1 hour, 2 minutes

2   meaty eggplants, with vertical stripes made on the skin with a peeler
2   summer squash
2   green zucchini
1   red onion
2   red, yellow, or orange bell peppers
12 carrots, peeled
4   garlic cloves, minced
1   cup olive oil
1   tablespoon table salt

1. Preheat the grill to 450°F. Cut the eggplants, squash, and zucchini into ½-inch slices. Cut the onion into thick disks that won't fall apart on the grill. Core, seed, and quarter the peppers.
2. Combine all the vegetables, including the peeled carrots, with the garlic, olive oil, and salt in a large bowl. Toss to coat the vegetables in the oil.
3. Grill for 45 minutes. Flip the vegetables a couple of times until tender, but not mushy.

SLOW-ROASTED RIB EYE, SLICED COLD

SERVES 6
HANDS-ON 12 minutes
TOTAL 3 days (includes chilling)

1   fresh rosemary sprig, stripped and finely chopped
1   tablespoon finely chopped thyme leaves
2   tablespoons finely chopped flat-leaf parsley
4   garlic cloves, finely chopped
2   tablespoons olive oil
2½   pounds boneless rib eye roast
1   tablespoon fine sea salt
Ground white pepper

1. In a small bowl, combine the herbs, garlic, and oil, then rub the mixture all over the beef. Place in a baking dish, cover, and refrigerate for up to 24 hours.
2. Preheat the oven to 375°F. Transfer the marinated beef to a roasting pan or onto a rimmed baking sheet, then rub with the salt and pepper.
3. Pop the beef into oven. After 15 minutes, turn the heat down to 325°F. Roast for 45 more minutes or until a thermometer inserted into thickest part of the rib eye reads 118°F. Remove the meat from the pan and let cool, uncovered, for at least 45 minutes.
4. Wrap in plastic; refrigerate for a couple of days before serving. Cut into ½-inch-thick slices and serve.

OLIVE OIL CAKE WITH BERRIES & CREAM

SERVES 6 (individual mini Bundts or 1 [10-inch] cake)
HANDS-ON 14 minutes
TOTAL 1 hour, 39 minutes

5   large eggs
1½   oranges, zested
1¼   cups sugar
2   cups extra-virgin olive oil
2⅛   cups cake flour, sifted
1   teaspoon fine sea salt
1   teaspoon baking powder
1   pint blueberries
Crème fraîche
Powdered sugar, mint leaves, for garnish

1. Preheat the oven to 325°F.
2. Place the eggs, zest, and sugar in a stand mixer fitted with the whisk attachment. Whisk on medium speed for 1 minute until evenly mixed. Reduce the speed to low and add the oil in a slow, steady stream.
3. In a bowl, stir together the dry ingredients, then add to the egg mixture in 3 batches, whisking at low speed throughout, just until batter is smooth and even.
4. Rub the inside of 6 mini Bundt cake pans with a film of olive oil and fill with the batter until the pan is nearly full.
5. Bake the mini Bundts for 25 minutes (or 10-inch cake for 50 minutes). The cake is done when a wooden pick inserted into the thickest part comes out clean.
6. Serve on individual plates with blueberries and a dollop of the crème fraîche. Garnish with the powdered sugar and mint leaves.

MIDSUMMER MEDITERRANEAN FETE

Ease into a summer state of mind, gathering friends for a light Mediterranean dinner party pairing of Old World deliciousness and New World savvy. The crowd-pleasing menu—from grilled skewers with tahini sauce to a whole-grain salad with a lemon-y dressing to a fruit salad with mint and tequila—glorifies seasonal flavors with a bright blast of fresh herbs and citrus.

APEROL SPRITZ
(PAGE 168); FREEKEH
SALAD WITH SWEET
LEMON DRESSING
(PAGE 171)

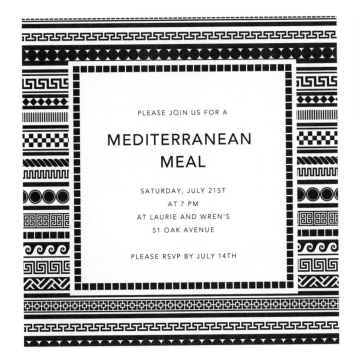

PLEASE JOIN US FOR A

MEDITERRANEAN MEAL

SATURDAY, JULY 21ST
AT 7 PM
AT LAURIE AND WREN'S
51 OAK AVENUE

PLEASE RSVP BY JULY 14TH

THE MENU

SIGNATURE DRINK: APEROL SPRITZ

SALAD: FREEKEH SALAD WITH SWEET LEMON DRESSING

MAIN DISH: JERUSALEM SPICED CHICKEN SKEWERS WITH GREEN TAHINI SAUCE

SIDE DISH: FROZEN FRUIT SALAD WITH MINT & TEQUILA

THE SCENE

INVITATION: An invitation in a Greek key pattern and iconic blue and white color palette beckons to good times in a setting where simplicity and sunshine reign.

DÉCOR: There is an unmistakable warmth and ease to Mediterranean hospitality. Repeat the classic palette of deep-sea blue and chalky white used on the invitation for your table. It will harmonize well with the emerald greens of the herbs and the pinks and rose reds of the produce featured in the menu. Select a patterned table runner and cloth napkins to match, while small arrangements of all white blooms, or cut herbs—mint, thyme, and rosemary—nestled into bud vases bring a natural touch and a wonderful fragrance to the table. Wooden cutting boards help delineate the serving space and bring one more natural element to the whole.

MENU: Mediterranean cooking blends the herbs, spices, and techniques of southern Europe, North Africa, and the Middle East. Fresh herbs define this menu, bringing a bright flavor to every dish. The skewered chicken kebabs, spiced with cumin and turmeric, are paired with a super-tasty tahini sauce packed with fresh cilantro and parsley. The whole-grain salad made with freekeh, a smoky, fire-roasted wheat, incorporates spicy, crunchy watermelon radishes, as well as the common Cherry Belle variety, and a dressing made from sweet lemon marmalade. Best of all, the fruit salad is bursting with zingy mint and a whisper of tequila and is made with frozen fruit right out of the bag to make prep super simple, but feel free to use fresh fruits if you prefer.

THE TAKE-HOME

Who can resist the hypnotic allure of an old-fashioned yo-yo? Set out unpainted wooden yo-yos and oil-based paint markers, and invite friends to decorate their own toys in delightful designs. (You might set out several sharp pencils, a ruler, and a simple geometrical stencil for guidance.)

THE COUNTDOWN

3 WEEKS: Send out invitations.

2 WEEKS: Order freekeh, if you can't find it locally. Find table-ware, serving bowls, linens, and cutting boards. Buy natural wooden yo-yos and paint pens.

1 WEEK: Shop for nonperishable cocktail ingredients.

3 DAYS: Make and refrigerate the tahini, minus the fresh herbs.

2 DAYS: Buy all fresh foods and flowers, and herbs, both to cook with and to decorate the table.

NIGHT BEFORE: Chill seltzer for the cocktails. Set up the cocktail station. Make the salad dressing. Arrange the flowers; set the table.

MORNING OF: Spice-coat the chicken. Chop herbs for the salad, tahini sauce, and the fruit salad. Add the herbs to the tahini sauce;

puree and chill. Cut grapefruit slices to garnish the cocktails, and juice grapefruits for the base.

2 HOURS: Cook the freekeh, but don't dress the salad yet.

1 HOUR: Make the fruit salad.

30 MINUTES: Grill the chicken, or wait until guests arrive, if you're gathering outdoors. Toss the salad.

20 MINUTES: Lay out the skewers, freekeh salad, and tahini sauce.

10 MINUTES: Set out ice for the cocktails and iced seltzer. Garnish the fruit salad.

5 MINUTES: Start the music, adding some Mediterranean flair, of course. Try something by legendary Egyptian surf guitarist Omar Khorshid or anything by Jordi Savall, a Catalan conductor and viol player.

THE SHORTCUT

AFTER THE CHICKEN PIECES are coated in the spice blend, the kebabs can be frozen until you're ready to grill them. Cut chicken pieces flat in order to prevent them from rolling on the grill.

IF YOU ARE FLUMMOXED by trying to find freekeh, substitute the grain farro, which has a similar texture, though a less smoky flavor.

USE STORE-BOUGHT GRAPEFRUIT JUICE in the cocktails instead of fresh-squeezed. Just be sure that there is no added sugar, and if it is still too sweet for your taste, add a little fresh lemon to the cocktail base.

THE POUR

Spritely and sophisticated, this effervescent low-alcohol cocktail is fizzy with a sweet-sour citrus bite, and an enticing rosy color. Best of all, it can be splashed together in a pitcher in no time.

APEROL SPRITZ

SERVES 14 to 16
HANDS-ON 5 minutes
TOTAL 5 minutes

1   bottle Aperol
1   bottle Prosecco
3   cups chilled seltzer
1/2 to 3/4 cup fresh grapefruit juice
Ice
Grapefruit slices, for garnish

In a pitcher, combine the Aperol, Prosecco, seltzer, and fresh grapefruit juice. Pour into ice-filled glasses and garnish each drink with a grapefruit slice or two.

FROZEN FRUIT SALAD
WITH MINT & TEQUILA
(PAGE 171)

JERUSALEM SPICED
CHICKEN SKEWERS WITH
GREEN TAHINI SAUCE

THE RECIPES

FREEKEH SALAD WITH SWEET LEMON DRESSING

MAKES 16 mini servings
HANDS-ON 15 minutes
TOTAL 30 minutes

FREEKEH SALAD

5 cups water
1 tablespoon plus 1 teaspoon kosher salt
2 cups uncooked freekeh (fire-roasted wheat), thoroughly rinsed
1 cup thinly sliced radishes (Cherry Belle and Watermelon varieties)
½ cup roughly chopped fresh cilantro
½ cup roughly chopped fresh flat-leaf parsley
½ cup roughly chopped fresh mint
2 red chile peppers, seeds removed, thinly sliced

DRESSING

3 tablespoons lemon marmalade
3 tablespoons extra-virgin olive oil
3 tablespoons fresh lemon juice (about 2 lemons)

1. MAKE THE FREEKEH SALAD: Bring the water and 1 tablespoon of the salt to a boil in a medium pot over high. Stir in the freekeh, reduce to a simmer, and cook until al dente, like pasta, 14 to 16 minutes. Skim off any foam as it cooks. Drain and rinse well under cold water; drain well.
2. Combine the freekeh, radishes, cilantro, parsley, mint, and chile peppers in a large bowl.
3. MAKE THE DRESSING: Whisk together the lemon marmalade, oil, and lemon juice in a small bowl.
4. Drizzle the dressing over the salad, sprinkle with the remaining 1 teaspoon salt; toss well to combine.

JERUSALEM SPICED CHICKEN SKEWERS WITH GREEN TAHINI SAUCE

MAKES 8 skewers
HANDS-ON 30 minutes
TOTAL 1 hour, 45 minutes

CHICKEN SKEWERS

½ cup ground cumin
¼ cup ground turmeric
¼ cup paprika
¼ cup kosher salt
2 tablespoons black pepper
2 pounds boneless, skinless chicken thighs, cut into 1½-inch cubes
¼ cup olive oil
8 reusable wooden skewers

GREEN TAHINI SAUCE

1 cup tahini
1 cup firmly packed fresh cilantro leaves
1 cup firmly packed fresh flat-leaf parsley leaves
¼ cup fresh lemon juice (about 2 lemons)
1 tablespoon chopped preserved lemon peel
1 teaspoon kosher salt
1 teaspoon black pepper
1 teaspoon paprika
1 garlic clove, finely chopped
½ cup water

1. MAKE THE CHICKEN SKEWERS: Stir together the cumin, turmeric, paprika, salt, and pepper.
2. Place the chicken, oil, and mixed spices in a ziplock plastic bag. Close the bag, shake well to coat, and chill for 1 hour.
3. Soak the wooden skewers in water 45 minutes.
4. MEANWHILE, MAKE THE GREEN TAHINI SAUCE: Puree the first 9 ingredients in a food processor until smooth. With the processor on, pour in the water in a slow, steady stream until smooth and creamy. Transfer to a serving dish.
5. Lightly grease the cooking grate of your grill, and heat the grill to high (450° to 550°F).
6. Thread the chicken onto the skewers and grill, covered, until charred, about 4 minutes. Turn the skewers over and grill, covered, until done, about 4 minutes. Serve with the tahini sauce.

FROZEN FRUIT SALAD WITH MINT & TEQUILA

SERVES 6
HANDS-ON 10 minutes
TOTAL 1 hour, 10 minutes

1 (16-ounce) package frozen sliced peaches
1 (10-ounce) package frozen chopped mango
1 (10-ounce) package frozen strawberries
1 (10-ounce) package frozen blueberries
¼ cup agave syrup
3 large fresh mint sprigs, plus ⅓ cup chopped fresh mint for garnish
1 tablespoon lemon zest, plus 2 tablespoons fresh juice (about 1 lemon)
2 tablespoons tequila (optional)

1. Combine all the ingredients except the chopped mint in a large bowl. Toss to coat; cover with plastic wrap. Let stand for 1 hour at room temperature before serving.
2. Discard the mint sprigs and sprinkle with the chopped mint.

BEACH HOUSE LUNCH

Can you hear the crash of the waves? Even if you are
nowhere near the shore, this outdoor party is nothing but
good vibes. The menu—fish sliders with fresh-cut slaw
and a slew of summery accompaniments—is stealthily
health-savvy in a way that never diminishes the fun, while
a few hours of concentrated party prep keeps any stress at
bay. Hang ten!

You're invited to a

beach house lunch

Sunday, August 12th
at 12:30 in the afternoon
The Brennans' beach house
16 Frasier Way
Santa Monica

Kindly reply by August 5th

THE MENU

SIGNATURE DRINK: STRAWBERRY-BASIL SANGRIA

MAIN DISH: SPICE-RUBBED FISH SLIDERS

SALAD: KALE, CHICKPEA, FENNEL & DATE SALAD

DESSERT: PEAR, GINGER & THYME TARTE TATIN

THE SCENE

DÉCOR: Look skyward as your inspiration, choosing a palette of blue in every hue from robin's egg to royal with a dash of midnight here and there. Shift into beach mode with napkin rings that give a nod to the traditional surfboard tether, made with snowy lengths of rope with their tips wrapped in life-preserver orange tape. Similarly, lightweight cording looks seaside-smart when wound around vases and votive candleholders, either discreetly tacked at the back with glue or fastened with a straight pin. A band of shocking orange or pink cord at the top adds a tangy pop.

FLOWERS: Sometimes using leaves alone makes the strongest statement, and never more so than when you choose supersized fronds from the philodendron family, including Xanadu leaves and those of *Monstera deliciosa*. These big-green beauties turn up the tropical vibe, and they're so intriguingly sculptural. Using two or three giant stems in simple, straight-sided vases works well. Drop them in and they arrange themselves.

MENU: There's nothing ho-hum about these fish sliders, seasoned with a delectable blend of spices and served with a mint-spiked slaw and a yogurt-based tartar sauce. They meet their match in a salad that blends sweet fennel, sharp kale, and creamy chickpeas, with a citrus-and-salt dressing that lets all that freshness shine. However, if your kale is less tender, dress it alone ahead of time—adding fennel and dates later—and allowing the citrus to mellow any particularly tough leaves. The only big waves here may come when flipping the *tarte tatin*. Just remember to turn the tart while it's still piping hot to avoid any caramelized fruit sticking to the pan.

THE TAKE-HOME

When was the last time you gave someone a friendship bracelet? Well, then, why not? Nothing says summer like these colorful, beachy accessories. Tie one onto each of your friends as a take-home surprise.

THE COUNTDOWN

3 WEEKS: Send out invitations.

2 WEEKS: Order tropical fronds and straight-sided vases online, or source through your florist. Buy friendship bracelets.

I WEEK: Purchase all non-perishable cocktail items and charcoal. Shop for tableware, flatware, glassware, and serving bowls. Buy cord, tape, and votive candleholders.

5 DAYS: Craft the napkin rings and, if desired, wrap the votive candleholders in cording as well.

2 DAYS: Shop for all the fresh ingredients, including the slider rolls. Put together the napkin and cutlery bundles.

DAY BEFORE: Set up the grill and the seating area. Arrange the tropical fronds in the vases. Chop the dates and walnuts for the salad. Make the simple syrup for the cocktails.

NIGHT BEFORE: Cook the chickpeas. Make the spice rub. Blend the cocktail base and chill.

MORNING OF: Assemble and bake the tart. Prep the slaw, but don't dress it yet. Set out the leaf arrangements.

3 HOURS: Cut up the oranges, slice the fennel, and chop the parsley for the salad. Make the tartar sauce. Spice-rub the fish for the sliders.

I HOUR: Garnish the tart with thyme. Light the grill, if using charcoal. Toast the rolls for extra crunch, if desired. Dress the slaw.

5 MINUTES: Set out ice for the cocktails. Light the votives. Toss the salad.

AS GUESTS ARRIVE: Grill the fish, and assemble the sliders.

THE POUR

This cooling sangria cocktail dazzles with a crisp rosé base and an unexpected whiff of basil.

STRAWBERRY-BASIL SANGRIA

SERVES 10
HANDS-ON 10 minutes
TOTAL 2 hours, 10 minutes (includes chilling)

1	pound fresh strawberries, quartered, plus more for garnish
2	oranges, sliced, plus more for garnish
3	bottles rosé
½	cup brandy
½	cup orange liqueur
½	cup simple syrup (see note for making simple syrup in recipe on page 160)
1	cup fresh basil leaves, plus more for garnish

1. Combine all the ingredients in a 6-quart container. Cover and chill 2 hours before serving.
2. Pour the sangria into a glass pitcher and serve over ice.

THE SHORTCUT

EVERY OUTDOOR PARTY is a collaboration with Mother Nature. Stock up on sunblock and set aside a few extra sun hats, as well as an extra shawl or two for the evening, to keep guests comfortable.

SWITCH FRESH FRUIT WITH FROZEN in making the cocktails—it won't dilute the mix as it melts.

USE HAY BALES COVERED IN BURLAP to fashion simple outdoor benches, complementing the laid-back look and keeping friends free from dampness, dirt, or sand.

GIVE GUESTS A SNACK, serving single portions of veggies with dip in short drinking glasses. Use a pastry bag to pipe the dip into the glasses and plunge in several long, lean vegetables.

PEAR, GINGER &
THYME TARTE TATIN
(PAGE 179)

THE RECIPES

SPICE-RUBBED FISH SLIDERS

SERVES 4
HANDS-ON 15 minutes
TOTAL 30 minutes

BONDI HARVEST SLIDER SLAW

2 cups coarsely shredded red cabbage
1 cup coarsely grated fennel bulb
1 green apple, coarsely grated
½ cup thinly sliced red onion
½ cup loosely packed fresh mint leaves
1 tablespoon roasted pumpkin seeds
¾ cup apple cider vinegar, plus 2 tablespoons
2½ tablespoons olive oil

SPICE RUB

1 teaspoon coriander seeds
2 cardamom pods (including seeds)
2 teaspoons sea salt
1 teaspoon black peppercorns
1 teaspoon smoked paprika
1 teaspoon garlic powder
1 teaspoon dried oregano
1 teaspoon chili powder

YOGURT TARTAR SAUCE

1 cup gherkins, coarsely chopped
1 cup plain Greek-style yogurt
¼ cup roughly chopped fresh flat-leaf parsley
¼ cup roughly chopped cilantro
2 tablespoons fresh lemon juice
1 tablespoon brined capers, drained and coarsely chopped
1 tablespoon Dijon mustard
¼ teaspoon kosher salt
⅛ teaspoon black pepper

FISH FILLETS

4 (4 to 6 ounces) boneless, skinless white fish fillets, such as halibut or grouper
4 sourdough or brioche rolls
1 tomato, sliced

1. Heat the grill to medium heat (350° to 450°F).

2. **MAKE THE SLAW:** In a large bowl, gently stir together the cabbage, fennel, apple, onion, mint, and pumpkin seeds. Place the vinegar and oil in a jar with a tight-fitting lid, seal, and shake until combined. Pour over the slaw and toss lightly. Set aside.

3. **MAKE THE SPICE RUB:** Cook the coriander seeds and cardamom pods in a small skillet over medium-high until lightly browned and fragrant, 2 to 3 minutes. Using a mortar and pestle or a spice grinder, grind together all the ingredients.

4. **MAKE THE YOGURT TARTAR SAUCE:** Stir together all the ingredients. Set aside.

5. **MAKE THE FISH:** Sprinkle each side of the fillets with ½ teaspoon of the spice rub (you can store the remaining rub in an airtight container at room temperature for up to 4 months). Grill the fish, covered, just until it begins to flake when poked with a sharp knife and is opaque in the center, 3 to 4 minutes on each side.

6. **ASSEMBLE THE SLIDERS:** Spread the tartar sauce on the bottom half of the rolls; top each with a tomato slice, 1 fillet, and a spoonful of slaw. Cover with the roll tops and serve.

SPICE-RUBBED FISH SLIDERS

KALE, CHICKPEA, FENNEL & DATE SALAD

KALE, CHICKPEA, FENNEL & DATE SALAD

SERVES 4
HANDS-ON 15 minutes
TOTAL 15 minutes

3   oranges
3   kale leaves, coarsely chopped
1   cup cooked chickpeas or drained and rinsed canned chickpeas
1   cup loosely packed fresh mint leaves
1   cup loosely packed fresh flat-leaf parsley
1   fennel bulb, trimmed and thinly sliced
7   tablespoons olive oil
1/4 teaspoon kosher salt
1/8 teaspoon black pepper
6   dates, quartered lengthwise
1/4 cup walnut halves (optional)

1. Peel and trim the ends of 2 of the oranges. Using a paring knife, cut along the membrane on both sides of each segment. Free the segments and place in a medium bowl, removing and discarding the seeds. Squeeze the juice from the third orange into a measuring cup to equal ¼ cup. Set aside.
2. Toss together the kale, chickpeas, mint, parsley, fennel, and orange segments in a large bowl.
3. Drizzle the kale mixture with the olive oil and orange juice, and sprinkle with the salt and pepper. Top with the dates and, if desired, walnut halves.

PEAR, GINGER & THYME TARTE TATIN

SERVES 8
HANDS-ON 20 minutes
TOTAL 1 hour, 10 minutes

5   ripe pears
3/4 cup granulated sugar
1   tablespoon lemon zest
1½   tablespoons fresh lemon juice
1   (½-inch) piece fresh ginger, peeled and finely chopped
2   tablespoons salted butter, diced
1   teaspoon fresh thyme leaves, plus more for garnish
½   (17.3-ounce) package frozen puff pastry sheets, thawed

1. Preheat the oven to 400°F.
2. Peel and core the pears; cut into quarters. Set aside.
3. Stir together the sugar, lemon zest, lemon juice, and ginger in a small bowl. Transfer the mixture to a 10-inch nonstick ovenproof skillet or tarte tatin pan. Cook over medium-low, stirring constantly, until the sugar dissolves, about 8 minutes. Increase the heat to medium. Cook until the sugar begins to caramelize and turns golden brown, about 7 to 10 minutes.
4. Arrange the pear slices over the sugar mixture, slightly overlapping the slices and filling the skillet. Scatter the butter pieces and thyme leaves over the pears. Cook over medium until the pears are crisp-tender, about 10 minutes. Remove the skillet from the heat; let stand while preparing the pastry.
5. Unroll the puff pastry sheet on a lightly floured surface, and cut out an 11-inch circle using a small knife. Place the pastry round over the caramelized pears, tucking the extra pastry beneath them.
6. Bake in the lower third of the oven until the pastry is golden brown, 30 to 35 minutes. Remove from the oven, and cool 10 minutes.
7. Place a large plate or cutting board on top of the skillet, and invert the tart. Garnish with the thyme leaves. Serve warm.

THE
RESOURCES

Even the most energetic host can lose steam when faced with a long shopping list. What's the fun of giving a tropical-theme cocktail party when you have to spend weeks hunting down coral branches for centerpieces? Or roaming from store to store in search of an imported Thai spice? We've included a range of shortcuts here to make entertaining as effortless as possible. For your reference, these pages include an insider's list, including purveyors of some of the most delicious food and the chicest décor resources from across the country. Everything here is available online or, in many instances, via phone order. These reputable companies offer everything from invitations to tableware to gourmet hors d'oeuvres and desserts, as well as hard-to-find ingredients and whimsical decorations. Just search by category, and let the fun begin.

INVITATIONS

BERNARD MAISNER
BERNARDMAISNER.COM
212-477-6776
Tabletop stationery, from hand-painted place cards and menu cards to divine invitations, all created by the internationally renowned New York calligrapher.

BRUSH & NIB STUDIO
BRUSHANDNIB.COM
Find exquisite hand-painted and hand-lettered custom invitations, announcements, menus, and more for any special occasion.

CRANE & CO.
CRANE.COM
800-268-2281
This classic stationery source offers stylish blank invitations, as well as ones that come printed when you type in your information. (You can also use their online templates to print them at home.)

MINTED
MINTED.COM
888-828-6468
A one-stop resource for invitations, thank you cards, announcements, party decorations, even home décor. It operates by offering crowd-sourced designs from independent artists around the world.

PAPER SOURCE
PAPERSOURCE.COM
888-727-3711
The company's do-it-yourself resources provide all the ingredients for creating a lovely invitation: paper, colorful backings, patterned paper sashes, and envelopes. Or leave the printing to the experts and receive the results by mail in about a week. (Rush service available.)

PAPERLESS POST
PAPERLESSPOST.COM
Brilliantly customizable online invitations that reflect a full range of styles and options.

PARCEL
SHOPPARCEL.COM
973-744-7700
Gilt embossed and gilded place cards and stationery with glittering warmth, as well as charming flat paper goods.

PETITE ALMA
PETITEALMA.COM
212-675-1610
Petite Alma's selection of birth announcements and baby shower invitations may be small, but the simple designs are irresistibly sweet.

SMYTHSON OF BOND STREET
SMYTHSON.COM
877-769-8476
The invitations and blank note cards from this British stationery company come in fashionable colors (red, cornflower blue, hot pink) and convey understated glamour.

SUGAR PAPER
SUGARPAPER.COM
310-451-7870
This Los Angeles maker specializes in customized invitations with a hip, energetic vibe and also sells fantastically chic place cards.

THE BAR

CRATE & BARREL
CRATEANDBARREL.COM
800-967-6696
This Web site is an easy source for all-purpose glassware, including two best-of-class offerings: the elegant Viv martini glass, $5 each, and the long-stemmed Camille wineglasses, around $13 each, an excellent universal wineglass.

FISHS EDDY
FISHSEDDY.COM
212-420-9020
Affordable glasses and bar accessories with a retro feel (much of the inventory consists of vintage pieces from old restaurants across the country), and good-looking, basic serving pieces include simple white olive boats for bar snacks.

IKEA
IKEA.COM
800-434-4532
Ikea has a wide selection of cocktail glasses and napkins. In addition, the great-looking wineglasses are so inexpensive ($4 each) you can buy them in bulk.

THE PANTRY

AMERICAN SPOON
SPOON.COM
888-735-6700
Try artisanal preserves in flavors such as blueberry lime, strawberry rhubarb, and wild thimbleberry, and fruit butters infused with ginger pear, pumpkin, and apricot.

ANSON MILLS
ANSONMILLS.COM
803-467-4122
Artisanal organic heirloom grains, produced with care at this South Carolina site; includes slow-roasted farro, and an exquisite selection of aromatic rices and polentas.

BONNIE'S JAMS
BONNIESJAMS.COM
617-714-5380
Wonderfully intense real jams (apricot-orange, coconut-mango), jellies (peach-pepper and fig), and preserves, all made from fresh fruits by this Boston-area jam maker.

DESERT PEPPER TRADING COMPANY
DESERTPEPPER.COM
888-472-5727
Bean dips, hot sauces, and salsas with extra Texas heat. Try the Peach Mango Salsa or the XXX Habanero Salsa.

EATALY
EATALY.COM
212-539-0833
Olive oils from Italy, Greece, and Spain, and dozens of authentic Italian pasta sauces, such as porcini and white truffles sauce, Ligurian pesto, and traditional marinara.

ILĀ
ILA-SHOP.CO
718-388-2510
This vendor sells globally curated home and kitchen goods from Brooklyn-based food and design community, Sunday Suppers.

THE OLD MILL
OLD-MILL.COM
865-428-0771
This Tennessee institution specializes in American heritage ingredients such as sorghum, grits, blackberry syrup, and pancakes.

PEANUT SHOP OF WILLIAMSBURG
THEPEANUTSHOP.COM
800-637-3268
Stock up on fresh, crunchy savories such as Indian cashews, Marcona almonds, and wasabi peanuts. For dessert, bring out the peanut brittle.

STONEWALL KITCHEN
STONEWALLKITCHEN.COM
800-826-1752
Purchase delicious jams, jellies, condiments, baking mixes, and other staples—including award-winning Wild Maine Blueberry Jam—from this acclaimed purveyor.

TRADER VIC'S
TRADERVICS.COM
925-675-6400
Their famous hot-buttered-rum batter makes a decadent old-fashioned cold-weather drink.

TRŪBEE HONEY
TRUBEEHONEY.COM
615-656-3174
Tiny jars of raw honey, like the ones used as sweet party favors in the Best Friends' Brunch (page 130).

UNIQUE PRETZEL BAKERY
UNIQUESPLITS.COM
888-477-5487
Keep these classic Pennsylvania hard pretzels on hand for impromptu parties. The company's most popular item, the six-pound variety pack, comes with jars of mustard for dipping.

HORS D'OEUVRES

DUFOUR PASTRY KITCHENS
DUFOURPASTRYKITCHENS.COM
800-439-1282
For gourmet bites, fill your freezer with these handmade, ready-to-bake appetizers, including wild mushroom phyllo triangles and Roquefort mascarpone puffs.

MACKENZIE LIMITED
MACKENZIELTD.COM
800-858-7100
This British food purveyor offers lobster palmiers, olives in puff pastry, and two kinds of rich, flaky Brie en croûte: mushroom garlic and apple pecan.

NANCY'S
NANCYS.COM
Fancy, high-quality frozen hors d'oeuvres such as mini quiches, crab cakes, plus more.

CHEESE

ARTISANAL PREMIUM CHEESE
ARTISANALCHEESE.COM
855-895-9255
The site lets you search dozens of artisanal cheeses by milk type, country of origin, or type of cheese. Also order gourmet cheese platters.

BEECHER'S HANDMADE CHEESE
BEECHERSHANDMADECHEESE.COM
877-907-1644
Find more than one dozen cheeses made with premium milk and no artificial preservatives, as well as cheesy side dishes, including gluten-free options, that ship frozen.

COWGIRL CREAMERY
COWGIRLCREAMERY.COM
866-433-7834
The gold standard in new wave American cheesemaking, this California purveyor sells some of the most modern and delectable cheeses. Order the classic collection online, which includes all their rich and creamy delights.

FORMAGGIO KITCHEN
FORMAGGIOKITCHEN.COM
888-212-3224
This Boston company specializes in rare cheeses from small farms around the world.

IGOURMET.COM
IGOURMET.COM
877-446-8763
Find hundreds of international cheeses and in-depth descriptions of each, including history, flavor, texture, and ideal food pairings.

MURRAY'S CHEESE
MURRAYSCHEESE.COM
888-692-4339
Browse more than 250 domestic and imported cheeses sold by this Greenwich Village institution.

ZINGERMAN'S
ZINGERMANS.COM
888-636-8162
This well-edited selection includes Zingerman's own handmade fresh cheeses as well as delicious, undiscovered artisanal varieties.

FRESH AND PREPARED MEATS

CHEFSHOP.COM
CHEFSHOP.COM
800-596-0885
This gourmet site is known for its incredibly moist, organic smoked whole turkeys, which are free of chemicals and artificial plumpers. Just warm in the oven and serve.

HAM I AM!
HAMIAM.COM
800-742-6426
These flavorful, not-too-salty hams (available with or without a pepper coating) have been smoked for 22 hours with real hickory wood. One ham serves 20 to 25 people.

JAMISON FARM
JAMISONFARM.COM
800-237-5262
The tender, low-fat lamb from this farm in Appalachia is free of antibiotics, herbicides, hormones, and pesticides.

KINGS RESTAURANT
KINGSBBQ.COM
800-332-6465
This company specializes in Eastern North Carolina's vinegar-based chopped pork barbecue (no heavy, gooey sauces), which it ships frozen. Order hush puppies and collard greens on the side.

LOBEL'S OF NEW YORK
LOBELS.COM
877-783-4512
Famous for its vast selection of hand-cut, never-frozen, dry-aged beef; all-natural lamb and veal; and rich, juicy, marbled Kurobuta pork (produced on small Midwestern farms).

NIMAN RANCH
NIMANRANCH.COM
In addition to selling the beef from its ranch in Marin County, California, in stores across the country, the company works with more than 600 independent farmers who produce beef, pork, and lamb from humanely raised animals.

NODINE'S SMOKEHOUSE
NODINESMOKEHOUSE.COM
800-222-2059
A reliable source for flavorful bacon, hams, and beef jerky, but most famous for its ready-to-eat apple-smoked pork loin.

NUESKE'S
NUESKES.COM
800-392-2266
The applewood-smoked ham is lean, meaty, and not too salty, and the homemade sausages (spicy chicken and Cheddar bratwurst are just two varieties) are perfect to throw on the grill.

THE SALT LICK

SALTLICKBBQ.COM
512-829-5285
Slow-cooked pork ribs, beef brisket, sausage, and smoked turkey breast shipped straight from the Hill Country of Texas.

SALUMI ARTISAN CURED MEATS

SALUMICUREDMEATS.COM
206-621-8772
Armandino Batali (father of chef Mario) uses old-fashioned Italian curing techniques to produce authentic salamis like spicy paprika and hot sopressata, and cured meats (coppa and lamb "prosciutto").

SMITHFIELD HAMS

SMITHFIELDMARKETPLACE.COM
888-741-2221
Home of the famously salty and pungent Smithfield ham, which is dry-salt cured, slowly hickory smoked, and aged for six months to one year. For a traditional Southern treat, slice it paper thin and serve on biscuits.

SNAKE RIVER FARMS

SNAKERIVERFARMS.COM
877-736-0193
Buttery, tender American-style Kobe beef, available in tenderloin, rib eye, and strip loin cuts, as well as boneless short ribs and hamburgers.

WILLIE BIRD TURKEYS

WILLIEBIRD.COM
877-494-5592
This operation has been producing its famous fresh and smoked free-range organic turkeys for more than 50 years.

SEAFOOD

CHEF JOHN FOLSE & COMPANY

JFOLSE.COM
225-644-6000
This Louisiana company ships fresh, seasonal seafood (crawfish tails, lump crab) but is best known for its tasty regional soups like Acadiana seafood gumbo and Creole corn-and-shrimp soup.

THE FRESH LOBSTER COMPANY

THEFRESHLOBSTERCOMPANY.COM
508-451-2467
Live lobsters, Rockport lobster bisque, and clambake gift baskets with the works: lobsters, clams, corn on the cob, lemon, butter, lobster crackers, bibs, and wipes.

HANCOCK GOURMET LOBSTER CO.

HANCOCKGOURMETLOBSTER.COM
800-552-0142
This Maine-based lobster specialist is famous for its Lobster Mac and Cheese and also offers other dishes made with its namesake food (and other seafoods), from fondue and stew to fresh sliders and beyond.

HARBOUR HOUSE CRABS

ILOVECRABS.COM
888-458-8272
This company ships succulent Maryland blue crabs—live or steamed and coated in secret seasoning—overnight. Order by the dozen, half bushel (three dozen) or bushel (six dozen).

JOE'S STONE CRAB

JOESSTONECRAB.COM
800-780-2722
Shipped overnight, this Miami restaurant's huge stone crab claws arrive cooked, chilled, and ready to be cracked open. Dip them in the company's signature creamy mustard sauce.

KELLEY'S KATCH CAVIAR

KELLEYSKATCH.COM
888-681-8565
For more than 30 years, this Tennessee company has harvested plump, briny, fresh (unpasteurized) domestic paddlefish caviar.

THE ORIGINAL CRABCAKE EXPRESS

CRABCAKEEXPRESS.COM
844-616-0575
These crab cakes are made from sweet blue crabs, contain no breadcrumbs or other fillers, and have never been cooked or frozen. They're sold and served at The Fenwick Crab House in Delaware.

RUSS & DAUGHTERS

RUSSANDDAUGHTERS.COM
212-475-4880
This New York classic stocks many varieties of impeccably smoked and cured salmon and seven kinds of imported and domestic caviar.

STERLING CAVIAR

STERLINGCAVIAR.COM
800-525-0333
This farm produces American sturgeon caviar that's as firm and flavorful as imported caviar.

SPECIALTY FOODS

CORN MAIDEN FOODS
CORNMAIDENFOODS.COM
310-784-0400
Handmade lard-free tamales from this company come in vegan, cheese, seafood, poultry, and meat varieties.

EARTHY DELIGHTS
EARTHY.COM
855-328-8732
Exotic wild mushrooms (shiitake, wood ear, enoki), dried mushrooms (morel, chanterelle, porcini), and truffles delivered overnight.

JOHNNY'S FINE FOODS
JOHNNYSFINEFOODS.COM
800-962-1462
Varieties of seasoning salts and savory salad dressings are this company's claim to fame.

KALUSTYAN'S
KALUSTYANS.COM
800-352-3451
This New York City specialty food store sells 100-plus flavors of chutney, including coconut, mango, ginger, and lime chili.

LUCY'S GRANOLA
LUCYSGRANOLA.COM
207-374-2251
Made in Maine, this granola is baked with local honey and maple syrup.

MEX GROCER.COM
MEXGROCER.COM
877-463-9476
Order everything from tortillas to specialty sauces and achiote paste through this online purveyor.

MUSTAPHA'S MEDITERRANEAN
MUSTAPHAS.COM
Here are gourmet products imported from Morocco, including green olives in cinnamon, preserved lemons, and beautiful jars of harissa.

PENZEYS SPICES
PENZEYS.COM
800-741-7787
The site sells more than 250 herbs, spices, and seasonings from around the world—scan the online index for detailed descriptions and recipe suggestions for each.

ZEE TEQUILA
ZEETEQUILA.COM
A full array of the most iconic—and lesser known—tequilas and mescals.

DESSERTS

BLUE BELL CREAMERIES
BLUEBELL.COM
979-836-7977
Texas ice cream famous for its fresh, homemade flavor—the company packs it in dry ice in a Styrofoam cooler and ships it overnight anywhere in the continental U.S.

CAPOGIRO GELATO ARTISANS
CAPOGIROGELATO.COM
215-897-9999
The site sells 250 rotating flavors produced every morning in small batches using only local, seasonal, or organic ingredients. A recent sampling: Champagne mango, salted bitter almond, and bananas Foster.

COCO SAVVY
COCOSAVVY.COM
Sparkling and delicate crystal-glazed edible flowers, including sugar-coated violas and pansies, can be pressed onto any iced treat. Similarly, dainty chocolates never looked so divine as when they come topped with a stunning combination of fresh herbs and petals.

DI CAMILLO BAKERY
DICAMILLOBAKERY.COM
800-634-4363
This 97-year-old company makes the best mail-order biscotti available (in eight signature varieties), and a bevy of other traditional Italian cookies and confections.

DIVINE DELIGHTS
DIVINEDELIGHTS.COM
800-443-2836
These beautiful iced petits fours and the addictive fresh apple tea cakes are perfect for any kind of shower or afternoon tea.

ELENI'S NEW YORK
ELENIS.COM
888-435-3647
Picture-perfect iced cookies custom ordered to work with any theme or palette. Eleni's shortbread, crisp and buttery, is a New York standard.

GEORGETOWN CUPCAKE
GEORGETOWNCUPCAKE.COM
888-502-7447
Classic perfection, these baked cupcakes are made with all the right stuff—such as Madagascar vanilla and Valrhona chocolate with decadent frostings to match, and flavors that change each month.

GOLD BELY
GOLDBELY.COM

Order signature desserts from New York's top pastry chefs, including Christina Tosi of Milk Bar, who sells her famously playful cakes, irresistible cornflake cookies, and home-baking mixes here.

LETTE MACARONS
LETTEMACARONS.COM
310-846-8029

L.A.'s stylish macaron makers create innovative, delicious flavor combinations to suit every taste, while their conical party tower, made with an assortment of 60 cookies, brings a bright, cheery touch to the dessert table.

LITTLE PIE COMPANY
LITTLEPIECOMPANY.COM
877-872-7437

This New York City bakery makes old-fashioned apple, cherry, and Key lime pies, plus over-the-top treats such as New York cheesecake with graham cracker crust and sour-cream apple-walnut pie.

MILES OF CHOCOLATE
MILESOFCHOCOLATE.COM
512-632-3323

These dense, fudgy brownies are as buttery and smooth as dark chocolate truffles and come in prebaked frozen blocks.

PAYARD
PAYARD.COM
212-995-0888

The Parisian-style, pastel macarons, made from ground almonds, sugar, and egg whites are crunchy on the outside and soft in the center and come in four flavors: vanilla, chocolate, strawberry, and coffee.

THREE TARTS
3TARTS.COM

This company's jam-filled petits fours have been known to send fans swooning. Check out the full range of bite-sized masterworks, from tarts and marshmallows to cookies.

CONFECTIONS

ALEXIS BONBONS
SWANSONVINEYARDS.COM
707-754-4018

These Napa Valley truffles, infused with dark chocolate and red wine, are the result of a collaboration between Swanson Vineyards and Vosges Haut-Chocolat.

CANDY WAREHOUSE
CANDYWAREHOUSE.COM
310-343-4099

Shop by color for candy to match your party palette, including black-and-white hard candy twists.

DYLAN'S CANDY BAR
DYLANSCANDYBAR.COM
866-939-5267

All sorts of classic and novelty confections, including M&Ms and Jelly Belly Candy (in dozens of colors) sold in bulk.

FINE & RAW CHOCOLATE
FINEANDRAW.COM
718-366-3633

Incredible chunky chocolate bars, some made with hazelnut butter or studded with habanero salt, and packaged in stylish paper wrappers.

MAST BROTHERS
MASTBROTHERS.COM

Ultra-fashionable confections from New York's famous chocolatiers. The online shop sells 12-bar collections of favorite flavors, as well as of-the-moment creations such as Rose & Sea Salt Caramels.

OLIVE & SINCLAIR
OLIVEANDSINCLAIR.COM
615-262-3007

Tennessee's best artisanal chocolates have a sweet Southern accent, including some made with cacao beans aged in bourbon barrels or smoked in a smokehouse, or blended with buttermilk.

RECCHIUTI CONFECTIONS
RECCHIUTICONFECTIONS.COM
800-500-3396

The couture confections from this San Francisco company include fleur de sel caramels, pâtes de fruits, and gorgeously imprinted fine chocolates.

VALERIE CONFECTIONS
VALERIECONFECTIONS.COM
888-706-1408

Next-level toffees, petits fours, and divine chocolates—some already prewrapped as party favors—made in Los Angeles.

WOODHOUSE CHOCOLATE
WOODHOUSECHOCOLATE.COM
800-966-3468

Gorgeous chocolates filled with exotic ingredients (Thai ginger, fresh mint, nutmeg, cloves), packaged in pretty pale-blue round boxes.

COFFEE, TEA, AND COCOA

BELLOCQ TEA ATELIER
BELLOCQ.COM
347-463-9231
Over 50 types of pure teas in various herbal offerings from around the world as well as in-house blends.

BLUE BOTTLE COFFEE
BLUEBOTTLECOFFEE.COM
(510) 653-3394
Committed to freshness and peak flavor, this coffee company sells brews and beans from their brick-and-mortar shops as well as online and also offers subscription plans to have your favorite coffees shipped to your door.

COMPARTÉS CHOCOLATIER
COMPARTES.COM
310-826-3380
This hip chocolate company founded in Los Angeles in 1950 has a celebrity cult following and is known for its chocolates' artful designs and delicious flavor. The products are customizable and ship throughout the world.

IN PURSUIT OF TEA
INPURSUITOFTEA.COM
866-878-3832
Many of the loose-leaf teas on this site come from small farms and collectives around the world and contain no added flavors, perfumes, or sweeteners.

LA COLOMBE
LACOLOMBE.COM
800-563-0860
Some of the country's pickiest chefs serve the five coffee blends from this company (including a rich, full-bodied decaf) in their restaurants.

MARIE BELLE
MARIEBELLE.COM
718-599-5515
Stock up on the best-selling Aztec Original hot chocolate, made from highly concentrated Venezuelan cocoa. Just stir in hot water or milk.

RISHI TEA
RISHI-TEA.COM
877-552-7977
A well-edited selection of black, green, white, oolong, chai, and yerba maté teas, as well as more than 30 caffeine-free botanical blends (including chrysanthemum, jasmine, and hibiscus).

STUMPTOWN COFFEE ROASTERS
STUMPTOWNCOFFEE.COM
855-711-3385
Purchase on site, order online, or subscribe to receive delicious coffees from this purveyor dedicated to harvesting the best beans from the best producers and to a meticulous roasting process.

UPTON TEA IMPORTS
UPTONTEA.COM
800 234-8327
Connoisseurs can scan the Web site for detailed flavor descriptions, then choose from more than 300 varieties of loose tea.

THE TABLETOP

ABC CARPET & HOME
ABCHOME.COM
646-602-3101
Some of the most exquisite table settings and linens come from this legendary and luxurious Manhattan design emporium.

CANVAS HOME
CANVASHOMESTORE.COM
212-461-1496
A vast colorful and creative shop full of modern designs adapted for the table, and including serving bowls and cake stands, vases, and carafes.

CROW CANYON HOME
CROWCANYONHOME.COM
800-777-0747
Known for its collection of spatterware, including both vintage and new items that work so well for eating outdoors.

FARM HOUSE POTTERY
FARMHOUSEPOTTERY.COM
802-774-8373
Gorgeously rustic American style for the table, including milk-glazed pottery, soft-washed table linens, and beechwood serving bowls.

IRONWOOD
IRONWOODBUILDVT.COM
This company's cutting boards make a simple, stylish serving tray, handmade in walnut and bright with graphic wedges of colorful paint.

LIBECO
LIBECOHOMESTORES.COM
This Belgian firm's hand-woven linens are the essence of good taste.

MERI MERI
SHOPMERIMERI.COM
650-508-2300
Playful swizzle sticks, as well as
paper straws, party napkins,
coasters, and popcorn boxes, all in
bright, fun prints and patterns.

MUD AUSTRALIA
MUDAUSTRALIA.COM
646-590-1964
Handmade porcelain bowls, plates,
platters, vases, carafes, and more
with a modern, streamlined design
and smooth, stone-like finish.

PARIS HOTEL BOUTIQUE
PARISHOTELBOUTIQUE.COM
415-305-7846
Unique heavy silver-plated pieces
(platters, trays, tureens, pitchers,
serving bowls, and teapots) from
places like the Waldorf Astoria
hotel in New York and the Hotel
Fontainebleau in Miami.

SUR LA TABLE
SURLATABLE.COM
800-243-0852
This site specializes in bright
tablewares and linens with a cozy,
French country touch.

THE DÉCOR

CB2
CB2.COM
800-606-6252
Our go-to source for so many
wonderful timeless, modernist
tablewares featured in this book,
from glasses and bar accessories
to serving pieces and vases.

JAMALI GARDEN
JAMALIGARDEN.COM
212-244-4025
An incredible resource for floral
design, offering a brilliant range
of vases and vessels as well as
tabletop topiaries, sheet moss,
miniature orchids, glass cloches,
and decorative faux mushrooms.

LEHMANNS
FLORALSUPPLIESANDMORE.COM
Browse the enormous selection of
natural-looking silk flowers. Even
the silk roses come in 10 shades.

THE MONOGRAM SHOP
THEMONOGRAMSHOPS.COM
631-329-3379
Have your name, initials, or address
printed (with crisp, preppy flair)
on colorful matchbooks, bags,
cocktail napkins, and more.

NEUE GALERIE
DESIGN SHOP
SHOP.NEUEGALERIE.ORG
212-628-6200
This retailer that sells everything
from furniture to lighting to serving
pieces is located inside the Ronald S.
Lauder museum in New York City.

RIBBONSHOP.COM
RIBBONSHOP.COM
607-754-5336
Miles of high-quality ribbons (both
plain and wire-edge) in every color
and pattern imaginable.

WORLD MARKET
WORLDMARKET.COM
877-967-5362
Candles galore—in every shape,
style, and color, both in wax
and LED. Also, find candleholders
here to perfectly suit any look.

THEME
ELEMENTS

FANCY FLOURS
FANCYFLOURS.COM
406-587-0118
These baking and decorating
products allow you to easily create
stunning cakes, cookies, or candies.

KNOT & BOW
KNOTANDBOW.COM
718-855-5393
Smart party supplies from balloons
and butcher's twine to confetti and
ombre beeswax candles.

LULU DK
LULUDK.COM
212-223-4234
Pretty, painterly temporary tattoos
designed to look like filigree jewelry.

M&J TRIMMING
MJTRIM.COM
800-965-8746
An extensive selection of decorative
trimmings, including imported
items, from buttons and accessories
to a variety of high-quality ribbons.

TOPS MALIBU
TOPSMALIBU.COM
808-828-0071
Party-perfect accessories, including
star-shaped sparklers to top a cake,
or gold-embossed crowns and tiaras
to top your guests.

32° NORTH
VINTAGE-ORNAMENTS.COM
760-487-8580
Source Dresden foils and trims for
New Year's Eve Cocktails (page 84)
and spun-cotton mushrooms for the
Woodland Baby Shower (page 146).

SPECIAL THANKS

CHEFS & TASTEMAKERS

Einat Admony Freekeh Salad with Sweet Lemon Dressing (p. 171); Jerusalem Spiced Chicken Skewers with Green Tahini Sauce (p. 171); Frozen Fruit Salad with Mint & Tequila (p. 171); **Jeremiah Bacon** Cornbread with Honey Butter & Scallions (p. 115); **Alexis Bittar** Caramelized Onion & Goat Cheese Tarts (p. 144); **Steven Escobar** Star-Spangled Smash (p. 104); **Frank Falcinelli & Frank Castronovo** Patio Punch (p. 161); Lemony Sardines (p. 163); **Marc Forgione** Mini Chili Lobster Rolls (p. 106); **Alex Guarnaschelli** Pavlova with Berries (p. 62); **Josh Habiger** Sweet Potato Pavé (p. 116); **Michael Hudman & Andrew Ticer** Carrots with Espresso, Dates, Sorghum & Lime (p. 114); **Donna Karan** Beet & Avocado Bruschetta (p. 60); **Sarabeth Levine** Two-Cheese Frittata with Arugula (p. 137);

Matt Lewis Sprinkle Layer Cake (p. 107); **Elisa Marshall** Virgin Berry Sangria (p. 96); Pea & Ricotta Tea Sandwiches (p. 98); Cheddar & Chive Soufflés (p. 98); **Seamus Mullen** Shaved Vegetable Salad with Parmigiano-Reggiano & Fresh Herbs (p. 60); **Jared Sadoian** Poet's Song (p. 134); **Bryan Schneider** Glühwein Sangria (p. 50); **Chris Shepherd** Roasted Green Beans & Okra with Caramelized Fish Sauce (p. 115); **Justin Smillie, Upland NYC and Upland Miami** Braised Chicken Legs with Spinach & Fennel Salad (p. 52); Individual Apple Crostatas (p. 53); **Alex Stupak** Passion Fruit Margarita (p. 124); Guacamole with Pistachios (p. 126); Green Herb Rice with Peas (p. 127); Chipotle-Roasted Baby Carrots with Watercress, Yogurt & Sesame (p. 127); Cochinita Pibil Tacos with Pickled Red Onions (p. 127)

PHOTOGRAPHERS

Stephen Baccon p. 172, 175, 177, 178, 179; **Stephen DeVries** p. 36; **Gentl & Hyers** p. 46, 51, 53, 110, 113, 114, 116, 117; **John Kernick** p. 156, 158, 160, 161, 162; **Johnny Miller** p. 14, 30, 34, 84, 95 (right), 96, 97, 99, 130, 132, 134, 138, 146, 151, back cover (left); **petrenkod/iStock/Getty Images Plus** p. 23; **Christopher Testani** p. 125, 126, 129; **Jonny Valiant** p. 27; **Romulo Yanes** p. 56, 58, 61

PROP SOURCES

Caspari, casparionline.com, Blue Splatterware paper luncheon napkins (p. 102, 105)

CB2, cb2.com, Drohgo taper candleholder (p. 145)

Chive, chive.com, Wave vase (p. 100, 107)

Neue Galerie Design Shop, shop. neuegalerie.org, Josef Hoffmann Wiener Werkstätte napkins & placemat (p. 24, 164, 166)

Red Clay Hot Sauce, redclayhotsauce. com, Bourbon Barrel Aged Hot Sauce (p. 120)

TrüBee Honey, trubeehoney.com, Honey jars (p. 30, 130, 136)

West Elm, westelm.com, Metallic & pastel glass candleholder & vase (p. 91)

The Tattooed Butterfly, www.etsy. com/shop/TheTattooedButterfly, Football coasters (p. 120)

INVITATION SOURCES

Brush & Nib Studio, brushandnib.com (p. 10, center, bottom envelope; 13; 92; 95)

Paperless Post, paperlesspost.com (p. 49, 57, 67, 77, 87, 103, 111, 123, 133, 141, 149, 159, 167, 175)

RECIPE INDEX